W9-AOL-821

COSTUME AND FASHION SOURCE BOOKS

# The 1980s and 1990s

Deirdre Clancy Steer

Produced for Chelsea House by Bailey Publishing Associates Ltd, 11a Woodlands, Hove BN3 6TJ, England

Project Manager: Patience Coster
Text Designer: Jane Hawkins
Picture Research: Shelley Noronha
Artist: Deirdre Clancy Steer

Library of Congress Cataloging-in-Publication Data
Clancy Steer, Deirdre.
  The 1980s and 1990s / Deirdre Clancy Steer.
    p. cm. -- (Costume and fashion source books)
  Includes index.
  ISBN 978-1-60413-386-8
  1. Clothing and dress--History--20th century. 2. Fashion--History--20th century. 3. Nineteen eighties. 4. Nineteen nineties. I. Title. II. Series.

GT596.C52 2009
391.009'04--dc22

                        2009006700

Chelsea House books are available at special discounts when purchased in bulk quantities for businesses, associations, institutions, or sales promotions. Please call our Special Sales Department in New York on (212) 967-8800 or (800) 322-8755. You can find Chelsea House on the World Wide Web at: http://www.chelseahouse.com.

Printed and bound in China

10 9 8 7 6 5 4 3 2 1

The publishers would like to thank the following for permission to reproduce their pictures: Corbis: 5 (Lynn Goldsmith), 7 (Pierre Vauthey/Corbis Sygma), 8, 9 (Pierre Vauthey/Corbis Sygma), 10 (Lynn Goldsmith), 13 (Bettmann), 18, 19 (Etienne George/Corbis Sygma), 21 (Vittoriano Rastelli), 26 (Vittoriano Rastelli), 28 and *title page* (CinemaPhoto), 29 (Yves Forestier/Corbis Sygma), 34 and 32 *detail* (Michael Ochs Archives), 35 (Benelux/zefa), 38 (Neal Preston), 40 and 36 *detail* (Michel Arnaud), 41 (Neal Preston), 44 and 42 *detail* (Albane Navizet/Kipa), 48 (Trapper Frank/Corbis Sygma), 51 (Neal Preston), 52 (Neal Preston), 53 (Mitchell Gerber), 54 and 52 *detail* (Karen Mason Blair), 57 (Henry Diltz), 58 (Floris Leeuwenberg), 59 (Reuters); Kobal Collection: 6 (Lorimar), 24 (20th Century Fox), 25 (20th Century Fox), 42 (TRI-STAR), 43 (MGM/United Artists), 47 (CIBY 2000), 49 (Warner Bros TV/Bright/Kauffman/Crane Pro), 50 (Darren Star Productions/Blakenhorn, Craig); Photofest: 30 (NBC); Rex Features: 12, 14, 16, 17, 20, 22, 23 and 20 *detail*, 32, 33, 36, 37, 45, 46, 56 and *contents page*; TopFoto: 27 (Hall & Oates/NBC/Photofest); www.somethingfine.co.uk: 12 detail, 24 detail.

# Contents

# Introduction

On January 20, 1981, the presidential candidate for the Republican Party, former movie actor Ronald Reagan, was sworn in as the fortieth president of the United States. Under Reagan, the country underwent a political and economic revolution characterized by deregulation (the lessening of government controls over the banking and industrial sectors) and large tax cuts. This political mood corresponded exactly to that of the then prime minister of Britain, Conservative Party leader Margaret Thatcher.

It may seem strange to preface a book on costume with a discussion about politics, but the way people dress is deeply influenced by the political climate in which they live. While liberal governments tend to inspire more adventurous, artistic styles of clothing, conservative governments, with their emphasis on the pre-eminence of the private sector, often produce fashions that reflect a sober, businesslike conformity.

This book examines the main costume and fashion trends in the United States and Europe during the 1980s and 1990s by drawing on the styles promoted by fashion designers and store catalogs and featured in movies and television programs of the time. It examines the world of couture—evident in fashion magazines such as *Vogue* and social picture magazines such as *People*—and, at the other end of the spectrum, the "street," where young people reflected popular culture by dressing in styles they created themselves. Theater and fashion students, re-enactors, and those interested in amateur dramatics will find inspiration here— whether costuming a group of 1980s "power dressers" or a 1990s "grunge" band.

*Below:* Any color, so long as it's black: in 1980 the American rock band Talking Heads start the decade as they mean to go on—by dressing dark.

## LOOKING TO THE FUTURE

*"We're on a road to nowhere,*
*Come on inside.*
*Takin' that ride to nowhere,*
*We'll take that ride.*

*I'm feelin' okay this mornin'*
*And you know,*
*We're on the road to paradise.*
*Here we go, here we go. "*

Talking Heads, "Road to Nowhere,"
1985

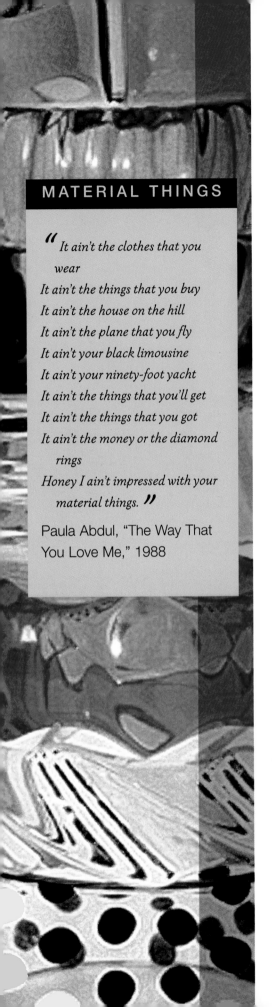

# CHAPTER 1

# Dressing Up and Dressing Down

## MATERIAL THINGS

*"It ain't the clothes that you wear*
*It ain't the things that you buy*
*It ain't the house on the hill*
*It ain't the plane that you fly*
*It ain't your black limousine*
*It ain't your ninety-foot yacht*
*It ain't the things that you'll get*
*It ain't the things that you got*
*It ain't the money or the diamond rings*
*Honey I ain't impressed with your material things. "*

Paula Abdul, "The Way That You Love Me," 1988

*Above:* American TV show *Dallas* both celebrated and critiqued the lives of members of a wealthy family in oil-rich Texas. The character of J. R. Ewing (Larry Hagman, far left) became an icon of 1980s greed and materialism.

## A MATERIAL WORLD

During the last two decades of the twentieth century, huge changes occurred in society at large. The 1980s were the era of materialism—the economy boomed, private businesses flourished, more women entered the world of work, and the acquisition of luxury consumer items became a desirable goal. An economic recession in the early 1990s forced people to curb their spending, but this period was relatively short-lived. Soon, the availability of cheap credit meant that people were spending as never before. Meanwhile, new methods of communication—computer technology, the World Wide Web, and the cell phone—affected the way people thought and related to one another, not to mention the way they shopped and dressed.

## THE STRANDS OF FASHION

In fashion terms, while the 1980s could be described as the era of excess, the 1990s were sometimes referred to as the "anti-fashion" decade, with subdued, minimalist styles that were a reaction against the materialism of the 1980s. Fashion itself could be said to move along in three separate strands, each one having its own rhythm. First, there was "high fashion," as seen in the catwalk shows of the top fashion designers, or couturiers, of New York, Paris, Milan, and London. Every season, the couturiers needed to produce something new and extreme to catch the eye of fashion journalists and photographers. The catwalk shows were also attended by a small number of very rich women who placed orders for the model dresses that appealed to them. These were then made up by the expert seamstresses in the couturier's atelier, or workroom. Store buyers also attended the collections, choosing the styles of clothes they felt would be popular with the more selective customers of the grander department stores.

However, the buyers also picked out garments with the potential to be mass-produced for "main street." This, the second strand of fashion, was made up of the clothes that ordinary people actually wore. But while strand two was influenced by strand one, its fashions changed much more slowly. For instance, you might say of a couture outfit: "That's a 1984 dress by Halston," referring, with an observation on

*Below:* A model wears a full-length ruffled dress from the Yves St. Laurent summer 1983 collection.

## MAKE IT—A 1980s JACKET

Buy an oversized jacket—there are still plenty to be found in thrift stores. Try to get one in a lightweight fabric and in the 1980s shape of the downward pointing triangle. Emphasize the shape by adding shoulder pads. These are available from fabric stores or you can make your own from polyester wadding stuffed inside pieces of lining fabric that match the color of the garment. Stitch in place at the points of the shoulders. Make the jacket fit over the hips by wrapping it more tightly over the body and moving the buttons to fit the new shape.

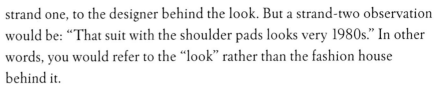

strand one, to the designer behind the look. But a strand-two observation would be: "That suit with the shoulder pads looks very 1980s." In other words, you would refer to the "look" rather than the fashion house behind it.

The third strand of fashion is a complex, ever-shifting group of what social anthropologist Ted Polhemus calls "style tribes." Almost all of us belong to a style tribe of some kind, even though we may think of ourselves as eccentric individualists. Sometimes the style of one fashionable group or another hits the mainstream. This occurred in the early 1990s with "grunge," and it appears to happen every five years or so with "bohemian chic." However, high fashion is what tends to change season by season, not the fashions of the style tribes.

While the fluctuating rules of high fashion, handed down from above by revered designers, may be straightforward, it's often difficult to remember what ordinary people wore and when they wore it. It can take about ten years to separate the main style of a decade from the mass of information that surrounds us. This makes the 1990s a difficult era to summarize—the dominant shapes are hard to discern when you're still in the middle of the confusion. The old saying "You can't see the forest for the trees" definitely applies here!

Apart from in a museum, fashion rarely exists in a vacuum—it's usually found attached to a human being. And fashion is the study of a person's character, which, when combined with a keen sense of period style, will give you a truly memorable costume. You can tell a lot about people from their style of dress, and a study of these different and quirky ways of dressing will make your pageant or drama richer and more interesting.

A good costume should tell you all kinds of things about the person wearing it. It will give you clues to obvious characteristics such as gender, age, and racial type but also to more subtle information such as financial and social status and occupation. Clothes can also reveal personality type: is the wearer a show-off or shy, is he or she sporty or a computer nerd, aggressive or gentle? Clearly, these observations can be difficult to make if everyone is

*Left:* In 1985, Dave Stewart (left) and Annie Lennox (right) of British pop group the Eurythmics experimented with styles embracing power suits and androgyny.

wearing jeans and T-shirts, but even then the hairstyle, the shape of the jeans, and the shoes will tell you a great deal.

## THE SHAPE OF THE 1980s

The prevailing shape of a decade often contrasts completely with the prevailing shape of the preceding ten years. The 1970s shape was characterized by narrow shoulders and the long, soft lines of flared pants and peasant skirts. The 1980s were the exact opposite—an inverted triangle with big shoulders tapering to narrow hips, topped by "big hair."

During the 1980s, women began to work in professions that had previously been dominated by men. To do so effectively, they needed to find a way of dressing that mirrored the masculine uniform of the dark, strictly tailored office suit. The new 1980s shape was a masculine look, with wide shoulders and slim hips. Dressing in this way helped give women a powerful "Don't mess with me—I'm just as tough as any man!" look, which was far removed from the slightly droopy styles of the 1970s. Dark colors, blouses and shirts with ties, hard purses with pointy corners, and killer heels all reinforced this need to be taken seriously in the workplace in an entirely new way.

Shoulder pads made a comeback in women's wear for the first time in forty years. The presence of little pads in the blouse, larger ones in the jacket, and enormous ones in the overcoat meant women could end up wearing three pairs of pads, one on top of the other. The effect could be that an ordinary woman looked like a football player.

*Right:* Padded shoulders were in evidence as early as 1980, as shown here in this jacket and skirt combination by French designer Pierre Cardin.

*Above:* With the short styles popular in the 1980s, hair was teased, gelled, and moussed upward to create a full effect. Brash, colorful jewelry completed the look.

## EVENING WEAR

However, even in the go-getting 1980s, most women didn't want to abandon their feminine side completely. Although evening wear echoed the new shape, the clothes also gave out a slick, well-groomed sexiness that was both worldly and decorative. Evening dresses were often made from stiff, shiny acetate taffeta, much decorated with beading or sequins. This decoration, previously done by hand at great cost, was now affordable thanks to inexpensive imports from the Far East.

Dresses in shiny satins and taffeta silks or polyesters were often constructed with attached bat-wing sleeves or with gathered set-in sleeves. Both styles had shoulder pads. Frequently, swathes of fabric were gathered and ruched onto hip bands or caught in with a stiffened basque flaring from the waist. Skirts were either tight and straight or asymmetric, draped, and swirling in silk, crepe de chine, or chiffon. To decorate your dress, you can buy beads, sequins, and ready-made sparkly motifs in craft stores to embellish the shoulders still more.

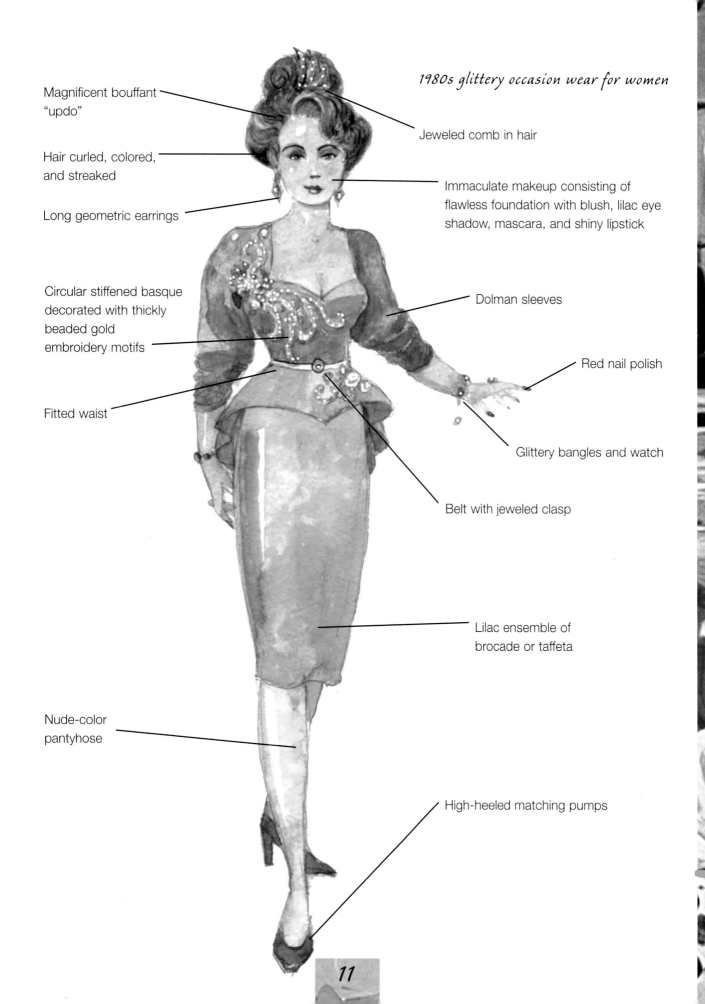

Magnificent bouffant "updo"

Jeweled comb in hair

Hair curled, colored, and streaked

Immaculate makeup consisting of flawless foundation with blush, lilac eye shadow, mascara, and shiny lipstick

Long geometric earrings

Circular stiffened basque decorated with thickly beaded gold embroidery motifs

Dolman sleeves

Red nail polish

Fitted waist

Glittery bangles and watch

Belt with jeweled clasp

Lilac ensemble of brocade or taffeta

Nude-color pantyhose

High-heeled matching pumps

# CHAPTER 2

# *Style Icons*

## PRESIDENTIAL STYLE

*"* I am delighted that these designers are being recognized for their incredible talent. It was an honor to wear each of these pieces, and every gown, dress, and suit brings back wonderful memories; moments in my life that I will remember and cherish forever. *"*

Nancy Reagan, speaking in 2008 about an exhibition featuring eighty of her most memorable outfits as first lady

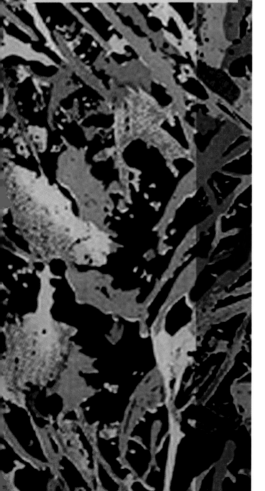

## JOAN COLLINS AND *DYNASTY*

The TV show *Dynasty* ran from 1980 until 1989 and was almost as famous for its parade of glamorous outfits as it was for its outrageous story lines. It was a saga about a wealthy but particularly dysfunctional family from Denver, Colorado. Actor Joan Collins, who joined the cast in 1981, privately claims to have designed most of her costumes herself. She certainly knew exactly what suited her, and costume designer Youcef Aden probably found it easier to allow Collins to have her own way. After all, if her appearance was at stake, she could be almost as fierce as Alexis Colby, her screen character!

*Below:* In *Dynasty*, the broad shoulders and nipped-in waist of this outfit accentuated Collins's figure and gave her character a domineering quality.

*Right:* Nancy Reagan wore a blue Adolfo dress and coat with gold accessories to husband Ronald's inauguration.

In *Dynasty*, Collins's tiny waist was shown off at every opportunity, and, to give the illusion of endless legs, she never appeared in less than 3-inch (7.6-cm) heels. Her evening wear for the show included glamorous silk jersey wraparound dresses, chiffon floor-length gowns with scooped necklines, and fitted bustiers—all with obligatory shoulder pads. For added mystery and sophistication, her character was often seen smoking black Nat Sherman cigarillos, a type of short, slim, luxury cigar.

## FIRST LADY OF FASHION

Nancy Reagan, first lady from 1981 to 1989, became an icon of American couture fashion from the moment of her husband's election to the presidency. A minute dress size 6, she made a point of wearing the creations of American designers with a refined eye for style. Such was her flair as a style icon that, in 1988, the Council of Fashion Designers of America presented her with its Lifetime Achievement Award. The three outfits she chose on the occasion of Ronald Reagan's inauguration ceremonies give a good idea of her taste and style. When her husband took the oath of office, she wore an electric blue outfit by Adolfo. The simply designed Melton cloth coat for the daytime events was brightened with gold buttons and a gold chain belt. It was worn over a matching collarless wool crepe dress with epaulettes and an off-the-face Breton hat. At the inaugural ball that night, she wore a slender, jeweled dress by James Galanos with a bolero top embroidered with multicolored stones. The skirt was beaded in a wiggly vermicelli pattern studded with crystals. Finally, at the presidential gala, she wore a showstopping red sheath of silk crepe with long sleeves and two buttons at each wrist, designed by Bill Blass.

## MARGARET THATCHER

When Prime Minister Margaret Thatcher first arrived at 10 Downing Street in 1979, her predeliction for pussycat bows and "garden party hats" made many people sneer at her public image. Soon, however, after centuries of male domination, the radical change signaled by the election to office of a woman prime minister was mirrored by a similarly momentous change in her wardrobe. Thatcher's aim was always to look

## IRON LADY

" Lady Thatcher wore her tailoring like a suit of armour. Her hair was as invincible as a helmet and her handbag as fearsome a weapon as any brandished by Boadicea [a warrior queen who fought against the Romans in England]. Such was the power of her handbag that it became a symbol of her style of government. 'Being handbagged' became shorthand for getting the sack. "

Hilary Alexander, writing in the *Daily Telegraph* newspaper

like a business executive, although she managed to be coolly feminine as well.

Marianne Abrahams, then design director of Aquascutum, the traditional English company that made most of Margaret Thatcher's clothes, said at the time: "She knows precisely what she wants and she's particular about the fit of the shoulders." Those "power shoulders" typified her style as much as the omnipresent pearls and round-toed Ferragamo pumps with sensible 1.3-inch (3.3-cm) heels. The tailored jacket and skirt were often in her preferred navy blue or sapphire, but she liked to vary the color scheme occasionally with fuchsia or cerise.

To achieve the Margaret Thatcher look, obtain a suit or dress and jacket in a good-quality cloth, perhaps in checked tweed or gleaming brocade. The trick is to combine elegance with a sense of purpose and a businesslike presence. Accessories should include a smart purse in dark leather, a single-strand pearl necklace, and matching circular clip-on earrings. Hair should be Carmen rolled, styled in a neat bouffant, and sprayed in place.

## PRINCESS DIANA

Diana, Princess of Wales, was easily the most influential fashion icon of the late twentieth century. Before her marriage to Prince Charles, Lady Diana Spencer dressed in the manner of the Sloane set she mixed with. (This group of upper-class young people was named for the fashionable Sloane Street in West London.) Diana liked to wear high-necked frilly ruffled blouses, pearls, calf-length floral skirts, loose short-sleeve shirts in Liberty-print cotton lawn, low-heeled shoes, simple dresses, and country tweed suits.

After her engagement to Charles, Diana began wearing more glamorous clothes and supported British designers such as Arabella Pollen, Bruce Oldfield, and Catherine Walker. Her shoulder-length, blow-dried, feathered-back hairstyle with its blonde highlights was copied by young women in offices worldwide.

Diana enjoyed wearing romantic ball gowns for the many state occasions she attended. One of her outfits, a full-skirted taffeta silk

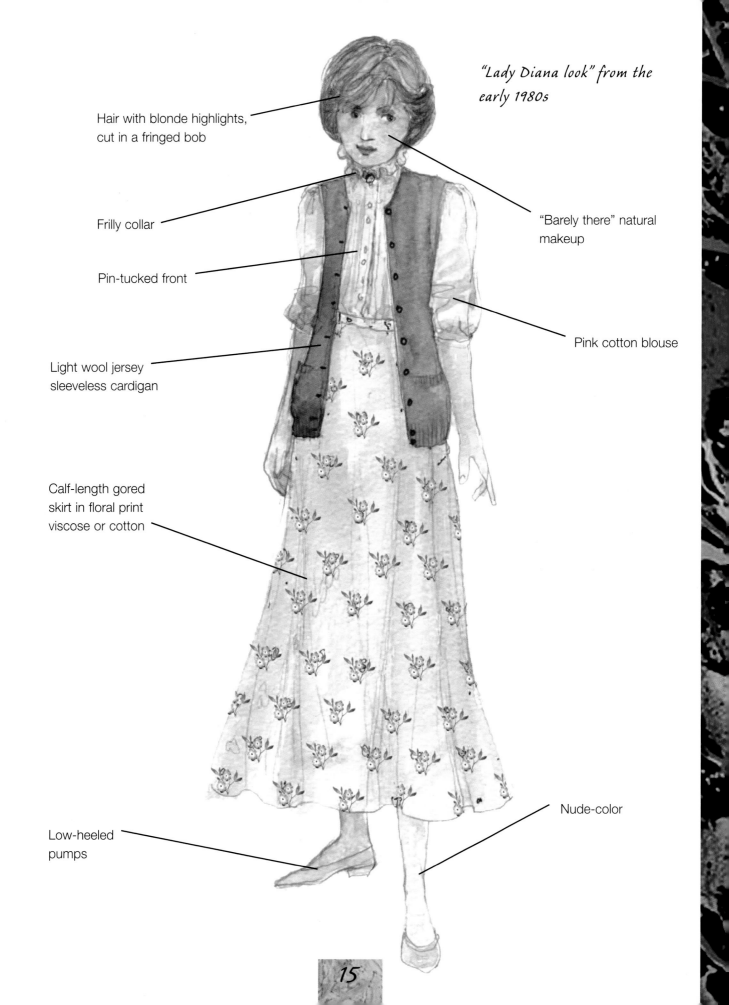

*"Lady Diana look" from the early 1980s*

Hair with blonde highlights, cut in a fringed bob

Frilly collar

Pin-tucked front

"Barely there" natural makeup

Pink cotton blouse

Light wool jersey sleeveless cardigan

Calf-length gored skirt in floral print viscose or cotton

Nude-color

Low-heeled pumps

*Above:* Princess Diana in one of the romantic taffeta silk ball gowns for which she became famous.

crinoline ball gown with puffed sleeves, was widely copied by stores such as Laura Ashley and became the classic dress style for bridesmaids from Essex to California for the next fifteen years.

As the 1980s progressed, Diana gained confidence in her own fashion sense and became more elegant as she began to understand what suited her. The tendency to wear frilled collars and full romantic skirts in sweet-pea colors gave way to a much sleeker look. In the late 1980s, as her marriage to the Prince of Wales became more troubled, Diana grew less dependent on the approval of her royal in-laws. Her dress style became more daring, and she started wearing clothes by international designers of her own choice, including Versace, Christian Lacroix, Ungaro, and Chanel. Her above-average height and model figure enabled her to carry off more extreme fashions.

Princess Diana's influence on the fashion scene was immense, especially in the 1980s, when her "fairy-tale princess" image was still intact. Her hats (particularly a little flat hat with a rolled brim decorated with a bunch of flowers and veiling at the back); her romantic evening dresses; her modest, printed-silk, calf-length summer dresses; and her simple suits were copied by manufacturers in every price range.

## MADONNA

Pop star Madonna has spent her career reinventing herself, her style of music, and her "look" in a way that no female artist has ever done before. In the late 1970s, the unofficial uniform of New York's dance students, of whom Madonna Louise Ciccone was one, included armfuls of rubber bracelets, crucifixes, torn T-shirts, pantyhose, and lacy brassieres. After signing her first singles deal with Sire Records in 1982, the budding pop star took the tattered look mainstream.

Since that time, Madonna has presented herself in dozens of different ways—as cowgirl, punk-in-a-kilt, vamp, virgin bride, and kitsch showgirl, to name but a few. For her 1991 Oscar appearance (performing the

Left: In 1985, Madonna's costume consisted of a black string vest and rubber bracelets—a look much imitated by schoolgirls at the time.

## STYLE TIP

To get the Madonna look c. 1981, you need to pair a customized T-shirt with the neck cut off and sleeves rolled up with a miniskirt. Wear this outfit with fingerless lace gloves, footless lace tights, and rubber bracelets. Makeup should include black eyeliner and red lipstick.

## HOLLYWOOD HEROES

"*Grace Kelly, Harlow, Jean*
*Picture of a beauty queen*
*Gene Kelly, Fred Astaire*
*Ginger Rogers, dance on air*

*They had style, they had grace*
*Rita Hayworth gave good face*
*Lauren, Katherine, Lana too*
*Bette Davis, we love you*

*Ladies with an attitude*
*Fellas that were in the mood*
*Don't just stand there, let's get to it*
*Strike a pose, there's nothing to it*

*Vogue, vogue.*"

Madonna, "Vogue," 1990

nominated song "Sooner or Later" from the movie *Dick Tracy*), Madonna wore a Marilyn Monroe-inspired Bob Mackie beaded white strapless body-hugging dress complete with fur and formal-length gloves. She was loaned $20 million worth of diamonds to accessorize the outfit. In 1996, Madonna's most critically successful film, *Evita*, the movie adaptation of Andrew Lloyd Webber's stage musical of the same name, was released. For years, Madonna had petitioned to take on the role of Argentina's Eva Perón, believing that this was a part she had been born to play. She transformed herself into the controversial figure of Perón by

wearing glamorous Christian Dior suits complete with red lipstick, her hair bleached and pulled back into a knot. Madonna also wore these 1940s dresses in real life for the duration of the movie.

## MALE ICONS

The mainstream role models of the 1980s were not exclusively female, however. The TV show *Miami Vice* had a huge influence on men's fashion and propelled two of its actors, Don Johnson and Philip Michael Thomas, to stardom. Johnson's pairing of a T-shirt under a suit jacket with white linen pants and loafers without socks was seen as the essence of "cool" by many young (and not-so-young) men. His unshaven appearance also sparked a minor trend for "designer stubble." The men's costumes in *Miami Vice* drew on an unusually feminine palette of pastel shades, including pink, blue, green, peach, and fuschia. During the show's five-year run, consumer demand for unconstructed blazers, shiny fabric jackets, and lighter pastels increased.

" The actors were little known before *Miami Vice* but soon became megastars. Don Johnson blew across the American consciousness, changing everything in his path. Men began sporting three-day stubble, espadrilles, and loafers without socks, Ray-Ban Wayfarer sunglasses, no belts, unconstructed Italian blazers over T-shirts, linen pants . . . And hey, as it turns out, pastels can be macho! "

From www.fiftiesweb.com

## THE RISE OF THE SUPERMODEL

In the early 1980s, fashion designers began advertising on television and billboards. Fashion models began to endorse products with their names as well as their faces, and a handful of them became familiar to the masses. By the 1990s, these "supermodels" had become global superstars. It has been said that the fame of these exotic creatures arose simply from "personality," because they appeared on talk shows, were featured in gossip columns, partied at the trendiest nightspots, and landed movie roles. But the "Trinity" of Linda Evangelista, Christy Turlington, and Naomi Campbell at their most powerful also embodied the physical ideals, the style of beauty—the spirit of the age.

In fact, the personal style of the supermodels wasn't a major part of their celebrity, at least not to begin with. They were, after all, fashion models, not character actors. Their job was to demonstrate and sell clothes, which they did extremely well. However, Linda, Christy, and

*Above:* Supermodels Christy Turlington, Naomi Campbell, and Linda Evangelista (left to right) pose together in 1994.

Naomi all had strong characters, which helped to make whatever they wore on the catwalk or magazine cover suddenly seem more interesting, more glamorous, more of the moment. They were hugely successful, and designers and magazine editors fought to employ them. The three women became "muses," inspiring fashion designers to do their best work, and, predictably, the fashion photographers and style press used this idea to make their fame ever more potent. However, by the mid-1990s the supermodel phenomenon was on the wane—the cult of the celebrity was about to take the fashion world by storm.

## CALLING THE SHOTS

*"We don't wake up for less than $10,000 a day."*

Linda Evangelista hints at the privileged nature of her life as a supermodel in *Vogue* magazine, 1990

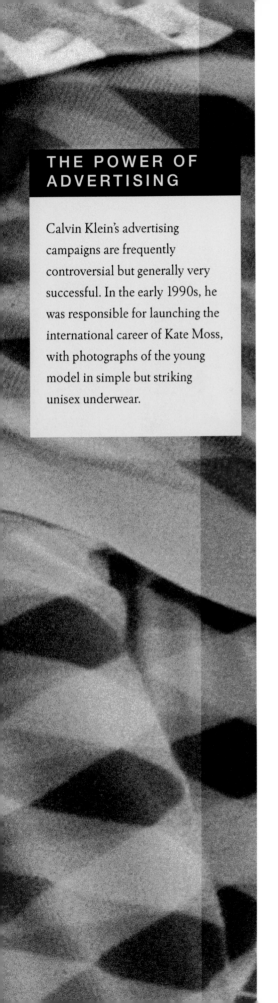

# CHAPTER 3

# International Fashion Design

## THE POWER OF ADVERTISING

Calvin Klein's advertising campaigns are frequently controversial but generally very successful. In the early 1990s, he was responsible for launching the international career of Kate Moss, with photographs of the young model in simple but striking unisex underwear.

## THE AMERICANS

American style had been defined earlier in the twentieth century by influential fashion designers such as Claire McArdell in the 1940s and Bonnie Cashin in the 1960s. Timeless, comfortable, and stylish garments formed the foundation of American high fashion as we know it. In the 1980s, American fashion abandoned its dependency on Paris, producing clothes that exactly fit the lifestyles of contemporary American women. Accessible yet stylish designers such as Bill Blass, Perry Ellis, Donna Karan (famous for her legendary "Seven Easy Pieces"), and Calvin Klein redefined how women dressed while for glamorous evening wear, Halston, Oscar de la Renta, and Blass could be relied on to make showstopping outfits of distinction.

*Above:* Neutral tones—Calvin Klein with models wearing his 1989–90 fall collection.

Perry Ellis, in particular, captured the mood of the time with his easy directional styles. They can still be found in home-sew pattern books and are simple to make as long as you observe the oversized proportions typical of the time. The unstructured suits (except for the inevitable shoulder pads), the big shirts, and the calf-length pleated skirts in easy-care fabrics such as soft cotton chambray or washed linen mixes suggested a straightforward, relaxed style that became the hallmark of American 1980s fashion.

Other significant designers included Dell'Olio for Anne Klein, the ultimate preppy lifestyle designer Ralph Lauren, and Norma Kamali. New York-based Kamali was known for her innovative designs, including a style of coat made from cut-up sleeping bags, her patented high-heeled sneakers, and her draped poly-jersey clothing. She designed garments for all occasions, from "lifestyle wear" to swimwear. Other trademark looks included pinstriped suits, poly-gab (Lycra-spandex) wear, and clothes made out of gold foil material. The most minimal of designers, Calvin Klein succeeded in reinventing a simple, cool way of dressing that depended on taking classic basic garments such as jeans, underpants, and crisp white shirts and, with a series of inspired advertising campaigns, turning them into must-have designer items.

## MILAN AND PARIS

You can enhance your costume re-creation by investigating some of the national differences in fashion styles that prevailed during the 1980s and 1990s. The Italian couturiers fell into two camps. Restrained elegance, soft tailoring, and subtlety of color and fabric were the hallmarks of Armani. For men in the 1980s, Armani's deconstructed suit, which took the stiffness out of traditional tailoring, was the uniform of choice for upscale office workers. Italian design also triumphed in women's evening wear: Valentino produced his signature red ball gowns, and Versace devised costumes of shiny fabrics that were flamboyant and theatrical. A liberal use of gold fabrics and revealing, body-sculpting lines ensured that nobody clad in Versace, or his slightly less expensive ready-to-wear line, Versus, went unnoticed.

Despite competition from Milan, Paris still considered itself the fashion capital of the world. Karl Lagerfeld was revitalizing the Chanel brand, often with witty tributes to Coco Chanel's historic, signature styles. The famous collarless suit in bright bouclé tweed, with its ribbon

## THE RALPH LAUREN LIFESTYLE

Ralph Lauren is the founder, designer, and chairman of a $900 million company. Not only was he the first fashion designer to have his own store, but he was also the first to sell the whole-lifestyle image that appealed to consumers worldwide. More than clothes and home furnishings, Lauren sells a lifestyle image of sophistication, "old money," and refined good taste.

*Right:* A fashion model wears a scarlet Versace ensemble on the streets of Milan, Italy, in 1982. Note the tapered pants, typical of the time.

*Left:* In the late 1980s, Yves St. Laurent's masculine look for women reflected the businesslike assertiveness of the age.

edging and matching silk camisole top, accessorized with oversized pearl and gold costume jewelry and little quilted purses on gilt chains, was newly fashionable and much loved by "ladies who lunch." Sometimes daughters wearing Lagerfeld/Chanel were seen dining with their mothers, who were wearing the original 1960s version of this long-lasting classic!

Perhaps the most iconic look of the 1980s, however, was created by Yves St. Laurent. He created women's day wear that borrowed heavily from men's classic clothing, using blazers, tuxedos, pants, and silk shirts. His evening clothes, on the other hand, were often romantically feminine, with beautiful "rich hippie" styling that used sumptuous color combinations and flamboyant layering. St. Laurent was the first major couturier to acknowledge that the fashion world could no longer rely on its haute couture collections by branching out into ready-to-wear with his very successful Rive Gauche line.

Another influential designer was Spanish-German-French Claude Montana. He produced some of the most theatrical clothes of the decade with enormous shoulders, draped leather, and helmets inspired by Japanese warriors. His more extreme outfits would have made good science-fiction film costumes. Montana also designed clothes for men under the Italian label Complice.

## LONDON

British fashion designers have a reputation for producing the most traditional clothes and the most cutting-edge fashions seemingly at the same time. British men's tailoring, thought by some to be the best in the world, uses super-fine wool cloth cut by hand and made into "bespoke" (custom-made) suits. Old-school craftsmen insist on at least two fittings with their clients, and the resulting garments can last for generations. Designers such as Belville Sassoon, Caroline Charles, and Jean Muir provided chic clothes for wealthy ladies, while stately veteran Hardy Amies continued to produce elaborate beaded creations for Queen Elizabeth and the Queen Mother until the end of the twentieth century.

At the other end of the spectrum, designer Vivienne Westwood's eccentric designs reflected her early experiences as a designer of "street" fashions for the 1970s punk rockers of London's King's Road. Westwood's

## MAKE IT— A MINI-CRINI

Buy five lengths of medium thickness basket-weaving cane from a craft shop, 6 yards (5.5 m) of 1-inch (2.5-cm)-wide curtain tape, and enough 2-inch (5-cm)-wide elastic to go round your waist as a belt. Cut eight lengths of curtain tape to the desired length of the mini-crini and attach to the belt at evenly spaced intervals. Thread the cane through the holes in the tape, completing the largest circle first at the hem. Keep threading circles of cane every 6 inches (15 cm) or so till you have created your mini-crini.

*Above:* Japanese designer Issey Miyake's loose jersey garments marked a radical departure from the formal tailoring seen in western fashion houses.

personal style was often more outrageous than her designs—pairing British classics such as the cardigan twinset with towering wedge heels, protest badges, clunky jewelry, and permed strawberry blond hair topped by a crown.

## THE JAPANESE DESIGNERS

In the 1980s, a group of Japanese fashion designers caused a stir with their often square-cut, asymmetrical, futuristic garments. Influenced by the principles of kimono-making and origami (paper folding), designers Matsuda, Issey Miyake, Yamamoto, and Kenzo invented a new style of clothing unlike anything the West had seen before. Although journalists praised the originality of these clothes, store buyers were nervous, describing the trend as "bag lady" fashion. Nevertheless, the clothes soon found success among Europe's more daring trendsetters and started to have an influence on mainstream fashion. At the end of the 1990s, European clothing companies such as OSKA and Completo Lino acknowledged the lasting influence of the Japanese designers by continuing to produce square, asymmetrically cut, layered clothes.

## STYLE TIP

You can create the Japanese look by the clever use of layers. Oversized crumpled leggings, kimono-shaped coats with huge attached scarves, T-shirts with cutout necks, and customized floppy wool cardigans will go some way toward getting this look on a budget.

## ORIGAMI WEAR

By the 1990s, Miyake and others were treating garments as pure art. Light, crisp, semi-transparent fabrics were pleated in a complex way that both molded the figure and disguised it, much like a modern ballet costume. Masks, sometimes with rabbit's ears in the same fabric, completed the look. The art of origami was clearly the inspiration here.

# 1980s and 1990s Day Wear

The 1980s witnessed the dismantling of social welfare systems on both sides of the Atlantic and an increase in the gap between rich and poor. Property prices rose: in some areas, the value of a home could double in six years. Young men and women flocked to where the money was, New York's Wall Street, and to jobs in advertising, with the goal of quickly earning as much as they could. These new business tycoons were known as young urban professionals, or yuppies. They took out huge mortgages at high interest rates and paid for home improvements with their credit cards (which also charged punishingly high interest rates). You needed to be a dinky (dual income, no kids yet) to stay ahead of the game in this new world. The "power couple" had come into being.

Men put away their 1970s flares and rediscovered the smartly tailored dark suit. Women, who were joining the urban white-collar workforce in

*Below: Working Girl* reframed the Cinderella story with 1980s career women in mind. In the movie, humble secretary Melanie Griffith blossoms into a quick-witted, business-minded executive.

increasing numbers, also decided that this was a garment that made them look assertive and professional. To begin with, only skirt suits were acceptable, but increasingly, crisply tailored pantsuits became popular. Power clothes could be found in every price range. Suitable outfits were available from Yves St. Laurent (who pioneered the pantsuit for women), from department stores such as Neiman Marcus, Bloomingdale's, Harrods, and Harvey Nichols, and even from discount stores such as Wal-Mart. Until the mid-1990s, the overwhelming color for women's office wear was black. The look was softened with a bright shirt-blouse or silk camisole. Matte black pantyhose, black low-heeled pumps, hard black leather or silver aluminum briefcases, and large day planners were the typical accessories. As computer technology progressed, the cell phone and laptop computer were added to this list.

## ALPHA MALES

Clothing for men in the 1980s expressed the conservative political climate with great accuracy. Neatly tailored dark suits were obligatory for traditional professions such as politics, law, and anything to do with commerce. Hippies and rock-star wannabes left over from the 1970s either went underground and adopted New Age spiritual values or cut

*Below :* The movie *Wall Street* (1987) told the tale of corruption and avarice in New York City's financial sector. With his razor-sharp clothes sense and the catchphrase "Greed is good," stockbroker Gordon Gekko (Michael Douglas, right) quickly became the role model for ruthless alpha males everywhere.

their hair, bought a suit, took out a gym membership, and signed up to the real business of the 1980s—the pursuit of large sums of money.

As modern centrally heated homes meant that there was no longer a need for thick tweed fabrics, two-piece men's suits were made in ever lighter weights. Shoulder pads increased in size throughout the 1980s and decreased throughout the 1990s until finally they were just big enough to define the shoulders. Inspired by *Miami Vice*, the bomber jacket re-emerged in the 1980s as a men's all-purpose outer garment, often with a fur fabric collar and football player's shoulder pads. (This shape was based on the airman's leather and sheepskin flying jacket from World War II.) Shirt collars grew smaller, seemingly overnight, and those 1970s patterned, flared pants and jeans, objects of great hilarity among the young and be-suited, were banished to the ever-increasing number of thrift shops. A decade later, they would be hunted down as desirable collectors' items.

By the 1990s, many men were no longer wearing suits to work, but for the more traditional professions, a good, sober navy or charcoal suit was obligatory. Away from the city, the countryside and suburbs were overrun with olive green waxed cotton jackets made by the old British country clothing company Barbour. In the United States, a checked shirt and a three-quarter-length hunting jacket were worn with combat boots or chino pants, together with mid-calf laced boots, a fur-lined cap with earflaps, or a Stetson hat.

## NEW MEN

The idea of the "new man" originated in the 1980s as that of the nurturing and emotionally sensitive male who was prepared to take on domestic chores and child-care duties alongside his female partner. However, many commentators believe that by the 1990s consumer society had remodeled this positive ideal of the new man solely along the lines of his shopping potential. Apart from occasional diaper changing, what really defined a new man was his brand of skin-care product, anti-perspirant stick, or hair gel. Because image was everything, the new man's clothing became all important.

*Left:* In the 1980s the world of work was a serious place, and nothing said this more than the understated yet expensive Armani suit.

The key to the new man look was informality. To this end, the men's overcoat took on a more relaxed form as a carefully designed all-season weather coat, often incorporating a fleecy zip-in liner for winter and a hood concealed in the collar. Originally designed for serious mountaineers, such garments infiltrated all levels of society and could even be seen worn over city suits on the streets of London and New York. For weekend wear, a "granddad" (collarless) shirt or polo shirt (a short-sleeve shirt made from mesh cotton and adorned on the chest with a logo) were commonplace. These would be worn with jeans and two- or even three-tone suede and leather walking boots. Formal wear consisted of black designer sunglasses, a tie-less shirt, a thin leather belt, stylish pants, and slip-on shoes, worn with a beautifully tailored jacket or blazer in a wide-lapeled, almost 1930s style. Medium-length hair was often gelled back.

*Above:* Pop music duo Daryl Hall and John Oates wear the alternative 1980s male uniform of beat-up leather jackets and jeans.

## JEANS WITH EVERYTHING

The word *jeans* comes from a material called *jean*, a tough, heavy cotton canvas with a twill or diagonal weave. The fabric is believed to have been named after sailors from Genoa in Italy because they wore clothes made from it. The word *denim* is derived from a French fabric—*serge de Nîmes*—serge (a kind of material) from Nîmes (a town in France).

In the 1980s, jeans became high-fashion clothing. Famous designers such as Gucci and Calvin Klein started making jeans with their own labels prominently displayed—sales skyrocketed. Denim also began to be used to make many other garments. The jean jacket was cut with a shoulder yoke, many seams, and a band on the upper hip; it was usually finished with snap studs and zippers and was worn by men and women. Women's pants were made in the latest designer shapes, such as the style cut with a fitted hip piece known as a basque and un-pressed pleats giving fullness over the hips but narrowing to the ankles. Skirts were soft and pleated or cut with six panels, and lengths varied from flowing multi-

*Above:* Stonewashed denim takes center stage in the 1987 TV show *21 Jump Street.*

seamed maxis that could be worn by women of all ages to the shortest minis adopted by the young. For men, short-sleeve plaid shirts, worn over a white T-shirt with chino pants, tapered to the ankle, became the only acceptable summer alternative to jeans. Chinos were basic U.S. Army fatigues and brought a welcome change from all that blue denim.

## NEW CUTS AND SHAPES

In the 1990s, there was a revival of the 1970s favorite hot pants. These were brief shorts, made either by cutting the legs off a pair of old jeans and artfully fraying the hems or buying them as ready-made garments. Although denim is never completely out of style, it certainly goes out of "fashion" from time to time. Younger people weren't particularly interested in Levi's 501s and other traditional jean styles, mainly because their parents were still wearing them. Since few teenagers would be caught dead wearing the same garment as their parents, they turned to fabrics other than denim and to new styles such as cargo pants, khakis, chinos, and brand-name sportswear. Denim was still used, but it had to be in different finishes; in new cuts, shapes, or styles; or in the form of aged, authentic, vintage jeans discovered in secondhand stores.

For men, women, and children, the major shoe of the 1980s and 1990s was the sneaker. Children pressured their parents until the desired, expensive (and therefore with a logo) brand of sneaker was purchased; failing that, acceptable knockoffs could be substituted. The tyranny of the sneaker continued until children decided that they were ready for Doc Marten boots. At this point in a young person's life, sneakers, although still ludicrously overdesigned and overpriced, stopped being an all-purpose fashion garment and were relegated for a few years to the sports field and the gym.

## DISPOSABLE FASHION

Only very wealthy women could afford to buy from the haute couture collections. However, by using the top designers for inspiration, fashion buyers could choose styles from the collections and have these adapted for mass production. The clothes would be made up by a huge labor pool of underpaid, usually immigrant garment workers at home or, increasingly, in the Far East. The garments would then be sold either in traditional stores or through a range of mail-order catalogs (eBay and online shopping didn't really take off until the twenty-first century).

In real terms, clothes had never been so cheap. It was possible to look fashionable and attractive on a daily basis for very little, as long as you were of average size and didn't want anything too unusual. The majority

## MAKE IT—A JEAN SKIRT

Take an old pair of denim jeans and carefully unpick the inside leg and crotch seams to 7 to 8 inches (18 to 20 cm) below the waist. Lay one leg over the other, both front and back, to form a skirt. Test for fit. Top-stitch the new seams in pale thread to match the original garment, cut the hem to the desired length, and either turn and hem with two or three rows of top stitching or cut and fray the raw edge.

*Below:* By the 1990s, some brands of sneaker had evolved into fluorescent works of art.

*Right:* An assortment of smart and casual 1990s day wear from the popular TV show *The Fresh Prince of Bel-Air*.

of people over the age of twenty-six went on with their lives in fairly simple, comfortable clothes usually bought from department stores, discount chains, shopping malls, or catalogs.

During the 1980s and for most of the 1990s, day wear consisted mostly of separates. The one-piece dress tended to be reserved for more formal events. This "mix-'n'-match" attitude had many obvious advantages. There was no need to buy a complete new outfit every time you went shopping. For instance, a favorite pair of jeans could be worn with anything from a vintage lace-trimmed top to a baggy sweatshirt, depending on the event.

Shopping by mail order became very popular since many people were unable to reach the well-stocked stores in the big cities and stores found it difficult and expensive to stock a complete range of items. Shopping catalogs were especially useful for garments such as plus-size clothing. Shoes, sporting and hunting clothes, home furnishings, and mainstream store selections and labels such as Bloomingdale's and Ralph Lauren could all be ordered from the catalog and delivered direct to your home.

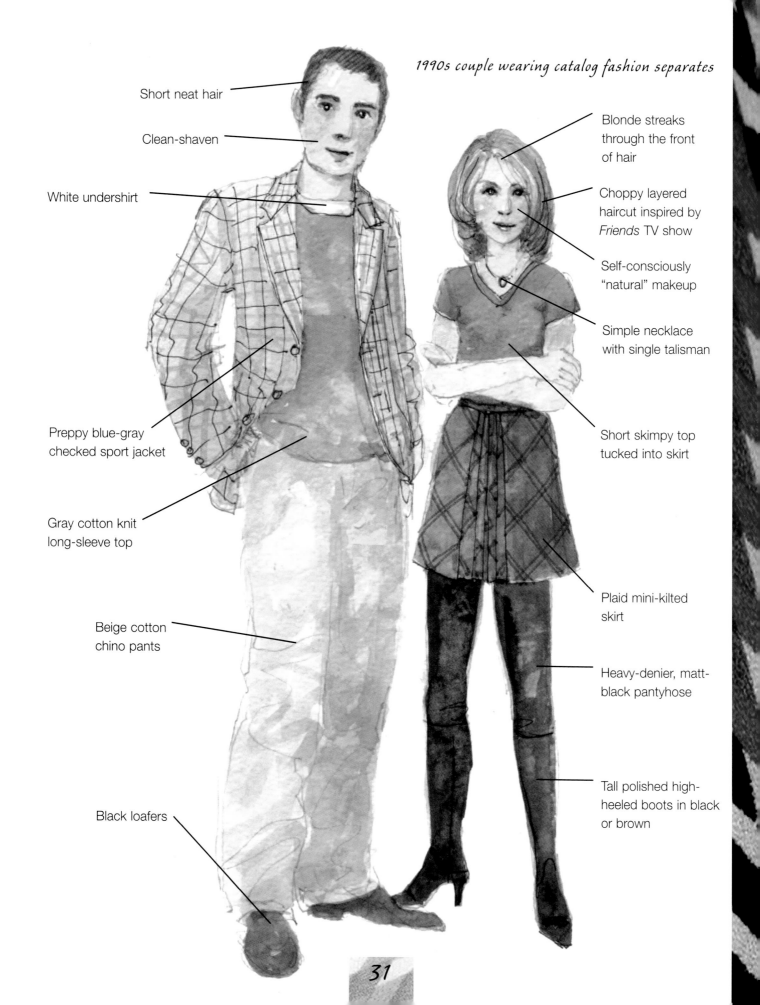

Short neat hair

Clean-shaven

1990s couple wearing catalog fashion separates

White undershirt

Blonde streaks through the front of hair

Choppy layered haircut inspired by *Friends* TV show

Self-consciously "natural" makeup

Simple necklace with single talisman

Preppy blue-gray checked sport jacket

Gray cotton knit long-sleeve top

Short skimpy top tucked into skirt

Plaid mini-kilted skirt

Beige cotton chino pants

Heavy-denier, matt-black pantyhose

Black loafers

Tall polished high-heeled boots in black or brown

# CHAPTER 5

# Sportswear and Leisure Wear

## THE FITNESS OBSESSION

For most of the twentieth century, the gymnasium had been a place frequented by serious sports enthusiasts such as boxers and bodybuilders. However, during the 1980s all this changed: as many

*Above:* The movie *Fame* and subsequent TV series of the same name (pictured) fueled a trend for sportswear and, most importantly, leg warmers.

workers' lives became more sedentary, people began visiting gyms to keep fit and lose weight. Membership of the newly carpeted gyms and sports clubs skyrocketed, and suddenly they were glamorous places to be. There was a dizzying list of activities to choose from. People began to "work out" using the many fitness machines now available—treadmills, step machines, muscle-group-specific bench presses of all kinds, and cycling and cross-country skiing simulators. A variety of fitness classes sprang up too, including yoga, martial arts, tai chi, step aerobics, and dance-based fitness. For those who disliked the sweaty camaraderie of the gym, a new breed of "personal trainer" would, at a price, come to your home to make sure you stuck to your personalized fitness program.

Not surprisingly, a whole new wardrobe of clothes was needed for all these activities. This was mostly based on spandex, Lycra, terry cloth, and increasingly elaborate designs of sneakers. For women, a welcome innovation in underwear was the sports bra. Increasingly designed as a streamlined outer garment, some versions of the sports bra had a "racer back," wide comfortable straps, and elastic under the bust. Lycra knee-length shorts or leggings, worn with short-sleeve or tank-top bodysuits, appeared in the more stylish gyms and fitness classes, and terry cloth bands on the head and wrists kept perspiration at bay.

One of the most successful movies of the early 1980s was *Flashdance* (1983), a Cinderella story about a young factory worker who wins a place at a prestigious dance school. Its influence, together with that of *Fame* (1980) and *Dirty Dancing* (1987), elevated sportswear and dance wear to new heights of popularity. This teen-focused, aerobics generation, with their slashed sweatshirts and leg warmers, took gym wear center stage.

## SHELL SUITS

Regarded by many as the biggest fashion crime of all time, the shell suit came into its own during the 1980s and early 1990s both as sportswear and as general leisure wear. This lightweight tracksuit

*Above:* The fashion for sportswear continued in the 1990s, with brand names such as Tommy Hilfiger.

### STYLE TIP

Get the *Fame* and *Flashdance* look with Lycra leggings, leg warmers, a bodysuit, a customized sweater or ripped sweatshirt, and a sweatband (all in complementary pastel shades, of course!).

Above: Originally designed as outdoor sportswear, brightly colored shell suits were soon being worn as fashion garments in the 1980s.

## THE SHELL SUIT

"The uses of a shell suit are infinite; whether it's performing record-breaking lunges, casually relaxing in fabric-clad heaven, or simply pondering the existence of the 'Golden Shell Suit,' the shell suit caters for all needs.... Owning a shell suit is like owning a pet or having a friend—they need looking after and kindness but with this you will be rewarded yourself....
Soon the shell suit and you will become inseparable. Although the clashing colors and shiny fabric will at first be daunting, you have to face your fears."

From the Web site
www.iloveshellsuits.com

consisted of a zip-front jacket and matching elasticized pants; both jacket and pants had an outer nylon shell, often bearing panels and flashes of different colors, and an inner cotton lining.

## UNDERWEAR

Although no professional model has worn a brassiere on the catwalk for the past twenty-five years, most women don't feel dressed without one. Today, the brassiere side of the underwear industry is a cross between functional engineering and glamour. Until 1980, it was almost impossible to buy a pretty bra in a larger size—anything over a 36C was liable to be a maternity item in easy-care cotton or a rigid pink one-piece foundation garment (soon to be made popular as ironic outerwear by some avant-garde designers). However, the manufacturers gradually responded to the inescapable fact that, despite the vogue for size-zero models, the average woman was getting bigger. This meant that by the end of the 1990s, many attractive, beautifully designed brassieres were available in all sizes and at all price levels.

In the 1980s and 1990s, while designers such as Janet Reger created exquisite underwear in silk and cotton lawn, modern fabrics such as Lycra net, spandex lace, nylon, and polyester were found to be far more efficient. The curved underwire made shelf brassieres with plunging cleavages possible, and plastic boning such as Rigeline was used for special-occasion long-line brassieres that could be worn without straps. Most brassieres came with matching underpants in all shapes—from boy-like boxer shorts to thongs—although many women preferred the comfort of pure cotton bikini briefs. Other items of underwear were the teddy, a hip-length slip that often included a built-in brassiere, and the bodysuit, a garment very similar to a one-piece swimsuit but with snap fasteners under the crotch.

## NIGHT WEAR

As far as night wear was concerned, anything would do in the 1980s and 1990s—from the glamour negligee to a boyfriend's old T-shirt. The silk nightdress with matching peignoir (dressing robe) so beloved of Hollywood movies still had a place in the wardrobe of a certain type of woman. For sleep, a simple T-shaped garment, often in cotton jersey and decorated with a logo or sleep-related pattern, was very popular, as it is to this day. Other women preferred traditional pajamas in soft Indian cotton or polyester satin. Undershirt and boxer shorts sets were also popular for their daring practicality. Those who liked to look more feminine in the bedroom wore reproduction vintage nightdresses in fine white cotton lawn.

*Below:* A relaxed approach to night wear in the 1990s meant mixing and matching and, often, sharing.

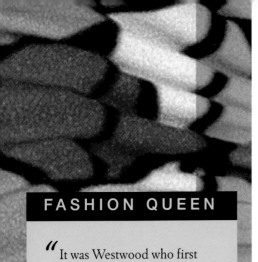

# Extreme Fashion and Style Tribes

## ON THE STREET

During the 1980s and 1990s, street style became more important than the old-style couturiers, whose grandiose designs seemed increasingly out of touch with most people. To keep up with rapid changes in style, clothing manufacturers began to employ "spotters" to find out and track what was being worn by young people at large, or "on the street."

*Below:* Punks adopted the Mohawk as an outward expression of their war against authority. The center strip of hair was dyed brilliant colors.

*Right:* New Romantics wore dramatic makeup and drew on historical themes as inspiration for their costumes.

## PUNKS

In American slang, the word *punk* means "inferior" or "worthless." Although fashion designers Vivienne Westwood and Malcolm McLaren didn't invent the word, they are certainly credited with inventing the style, and McLaren went on to create the British band the Sex Pistols as part of his rebellious punk vision. Although it was a 1970s style tribe movement, punk strongly influenced 1980s fashion and endured well into that decade. The punks' belief system was nihilistic (believing in nothing), and the enraged chant of, "No future!" was their rallying cry. Among other things, punk was a reaction against the "peace and love" message of the 1970s hippie culture (which itself was a revolt against the attitudes of an earlier generation born out of two world wars). Punk expressed the frustration of young people for whom economic stagnation and rising unemployment had become a part of everyday life. Punks took black leather, grubby T-shirts, drainpipe pants, and black trash bags and combined them with Doc Marten boots, chains, and safety pins to create an aggressive, posturing demeanor. Most noticeable of all, however, was the hair. The scalp was often shaved except for a Mohawk-style crest running from the brow to the nape of the neck. This crest was bleached, dyed a bright rainbow color, then gelled into a rigid fan that startled and shocked the casual observer.

## NEW ROMANTICS

A fashion trend of the early 1980s, New Romanticism grew out of 1970s "glam rock." Its followers dressed in androgynous clothing and wore dramatic cosmetics inspired by the earlier punk fashions and the creative imaginings of art school students. Men wore frilly "fop" shirts or exaggerated versions of upscale, tailored fashion; they often dressed their hair in a gelled quiff and used large amounts of eye makeup. Pop stars David Bowie and Brian Eno influenced this style, and pop bands such as Spandau Ballet, Depeche Mode, and Culture Club grew out of the New Romantic movement. The trend was quickly seized by commercial forces and watered-down versions of the clothing were cheaply reproduced for the general public.

## PUFFY SHIRTS

In 1981, Vivienne Westwood's pirate collection made its mark on the fashion and music industries. Her take on the New Romantic look, complete with colorful makeup and flowing outfits, swept through London. Shirts with girly ruffles are still evident in today's boho chic styles. In the 1990s, an episode of the comedy TV show *Seinfeld* titled "The Puffy Shirt" wryly illustrated the embarrassment such a garment could cause.

## GOTHS

Goths have had remarkable staying power as a style tribe, lasting well into the twenty-first century. The inspirations of Dracula, vampires, and TV shows such as *The Addams Family* and *The Munsters* have produced some remarkable goth variants, many of them driven by a strong mystical philosophy. The color for clothes is black, black, and more black; the fabrics are velvet, lace, and leather with corsets, silver jewelry, and spiky-heeled shoes or boots. Makeup for both sexes consists of white pancake for skin with theatrical black-and-purple eyes and lips. The black-dyed hair is teased upward as far as it will go (hers) or gelled flat with a shaved or painted widow's peak (his).

## BIKERS AND ROCK CHICKS

Another subculture of the 1980s and 1990s was that of the biker, whose costume was based on black leather, denim, and metal. The male biker dressed almost entirely in black. The leather jacket was often customized with images such as death's head masks or wings worked in steel studs.

*Below:* In 1990, some of the band members who had been at the forefront of the punk movement in New York City in the 1970s went on tour again, wearing an eclectic mix of flamboyant zoot suits and rocker clothing.

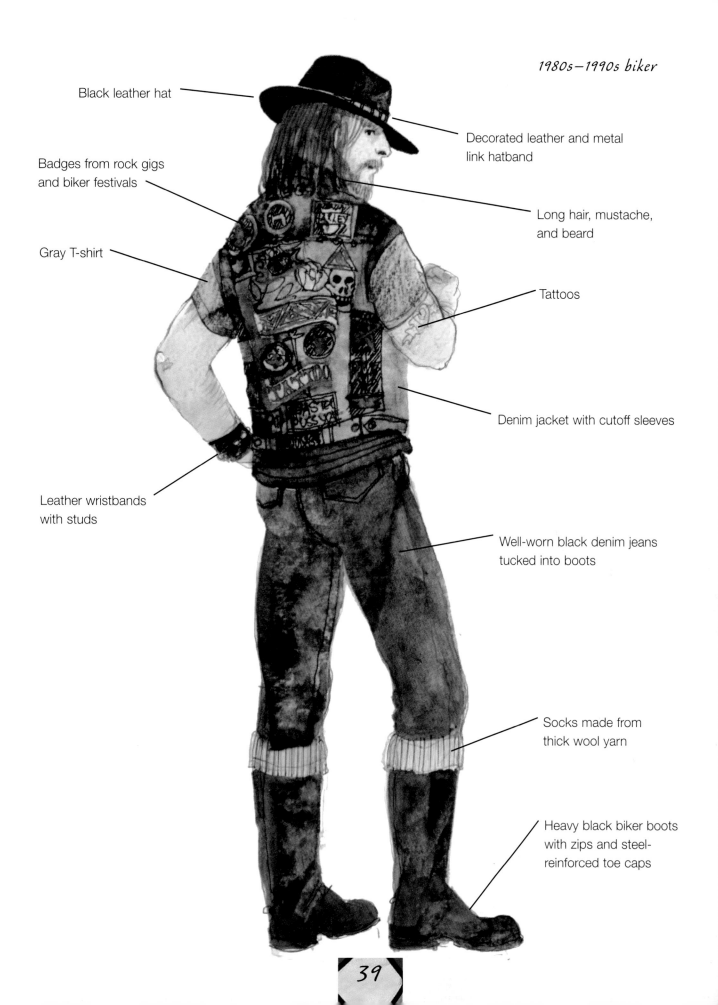

Black leather hat

Decorated leather and metal link hatband

Badges from rock gigs and biker festivals

Long hair, mustache, and beard

Gray T-shirt

Tattoos

Denim jacket with cutoff sleeves

Leather wristbands with studs

Well-worn black denim jeans tucked into boots

Socks made from thick wool yarn

Heavy black biker boots with zips and steel-reinforced toe caps

In 1997, American designer Lawrence Steele placed a startling advertisement in *Elle* magazine. It featured an androgynous-looking model, with her skin waxed and oiled, wearing a gold-sequinned G-string, high strappy sandals, and a black PVC trench coat. Her hair was gelled into an extreme updo, pasted flat to the sides of the head and sticking up in spikes on top. Heavy eye makeup and a fierce expression completed the look.

When it came to actually riding a motorcycle, rather than simply posing, bikers would wear tight leather pants with ridged protective padding at the knee and waist. The heavy boots had steel toe caps for protection as well as display. Accessories included heavy gauntlet gloves and, around the neck, a red or black and red cotton bandanna, which could be pulled up to keep the nose and mouth free of dust. When not on the road, a biker would wear a sleeveless denim jacket adorned with many badges that had been collected over the years. A Stetson hat sometimes replaced the helmet, black denim jeans substituted for the leather pants, and a white or gray T-shirt and bandanna completed the look.

Girl bikers and rock chicks often wore the same jacket as their men. Tight leather short skirts were sometimes worn instead of pants, and the T-shirt was often replaced by a skintight, leopard-print top with a waist-cinching belt. Heavy biker boots were worn, but it's also possible to find stiletto-heeled biker boots in some specialty stores. Big dangly earrings and a huge back-combed peroxided beehive hairdo were essential elements of this style.

## CATWALK CRAZINESS

Throughout the 1980s and 1990s, the catwalk shows became more and more outlandish, with the designers spending tens of thousands of dollars to mount what were, in effect, theatrical events. Hair was dressed in extreme shapes, sometimes decked with peculiar extensions or themed headpieces, and makeup was especially created for maximum impact and resembled nothing that anyone might ordinarily wear. The models became ever taller, younger, and thinner, stalking the runways with a special "dragged from the hip" walk, wearing the fiercest of scowls (and sometimes not much else). Fashion designers John Galliano and Jean Paul Gaultier, in particular, introduced partial nudity into their shows; anything to excite the fashion photographers and obtain that essential press coverage. Behind the scenes, the powerful store buyers often attended private showings of the garments that they actually intended to purchase, stripped of all the catwalk silliness.

*Left:* Westwood's mini-crini combined the ballet dancer's tutu with a shortened version of the Victorian crinoline. The garment moved and swayed as the wearer walked.

*Right:* Madonna wearing the Blonde Ambition corset in pink satin, designed by Jean Paul Gaultier.

Nevertheless, if you're looking for a dramatic outfit to illustrate the height of 1980s or 1990s extreme fashion, then the catwalk is an essential reference point.

## UNDERWEAR AS OUTERWEAR

In 1987, Vivienne Westwood designed a "Statue of Liberty" corset in the British wool Harris tweed. It was the first corset to be introduced as outerwear. Later Westwood collections featured beautifully cut eighteenth-century-style corsets in velvet and in an oversized print of a painting by eighteenth-century French artist François Boucher. Versions of this corset design were very popular and became the point of departure for many wedding and evening dresses.

Gaultier also exploited the idea of using underwear as high fashion. He seemed to be particularly fascinated by the Band-Aid-pink corsets of the 1950s and 1960s, which had been popular with middle-aged women who felt that their foundation garments needed serious structural engineering. These "corselettes" had had sturdy straps, suspenders to hold up the stockings, torpedo-shaped breast support sections, and much top stitching. Gaultier created an armor-like corset for Madonna's Blonde Ambition tour that exaggerated the circle-stitched shape with outrageous 6-inch (15-cm) cone breasts. The tour featured these garments in shiny pink silk satin, in gold lamé, and, with added splits and straps, in black leather. At a party or a pageant, such an ensemble would be very memorable.

Gaultier wasn't the only designer to explore this trend: Valentino's evening dress of red chiffon and quilted satin featured the corset as a kind of armor, and in 1991–2, Yves St. Laurent created corset dresses based on the twentieth-century girdle. Another item of underwear, the camisole, also migrated outward as a pretty and useful top that could be worn under jackets, where a blouse would look too fussy. Antique lace-edged petticoats were worn as skirts—after all, they were far too attractive to keep hidden. However, this use of vintage pieces tended to be a quirky choice by independent-minded young women on a limited budget rather than part of mainstream fashion.

## GAULTIER

Jean Paul Gaultier's clothes transcend the traditional boundaries of gender and fashion. He is famous for having brought high fashion to the masses and street style to the catwalk, most notably in the shape of skirts for men and underwear as outerwear. Since 1976, his themed collections have drawn inspiration from the most eclectic sources, from French cultural icons to the London street scene.

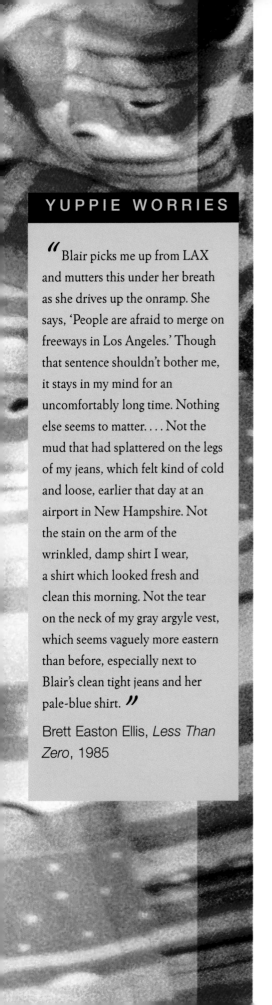

# CHAPTER 7
# *The Media and Celebrity Culture*

## THE BRAT PACK

During the 1980s, a series of Hollywood movies aimed at the teenage market seized the imagination of a generation. Movies such as *The Breakfast Club*, *St. Elmo's Fire*, and *Pretty in Pink* featured misfits in skinny ties and prom queens wearing frosted lip gloss and made stars of

*Above:* Brat Pack members included (left to right) Elizabeth Perkins, Demi Moore, and Rob Lowe. Actor James Belushi stands behind them.

a group of young actors who became known as the Brat Pack. Young people everywhere rushed to copy the clean-cut, all-American looks of Demi Moore, Molly Ringwald, Ally Sheedy, Rob Lowe, and Judd Nelson. With their yuppie styling and sporting designer jeans and cool shades, these spoiled and often self-indulgent celebrities encapsulated the spirit of 1980s individualism. In contrast to the hippie generation before them, they made it fashionable to possess wealth and privilege.

## A NEW LIFESTYLE

As more women entered the workforce in the 1980s, many of the traditional attitudes toward male and female roles within the family began to change. Between 1987 and 1991, the TV series *thirtysomething* charted the domestic and professional lives of a group of friends living in Philadelphia. It examined their personal relationships, love affairs, and experiences as parents of small children.

Rather than relying on the framework of a conventional nuclear family, these friends depended on one another for support. Their clothes were both preppy and casual, reflecting their career-focused but caring outlook. They ranged from men's suits worn with open-necked shirts (for the advertising executive and graphic designer characters) to the wackier hippie-type outfits, such as blanket coats, worn by one of the female characters (a photographer.) The lifestyle the show depicted had a powerful impact on the makers of TV advertisements, who mimicked its tone. These advertisements, in turn, influenced what people bought, how they dressed, and the way they decorated their homes.

*Above: thirtysomething* looked at suburban life and at the conflicts involved in juggling careers and family. The costumes reflected the tastes of a generation who had grown up during the hippie era but found themselves at the center of 1980s yuppie culture.

## YUMMY MOMMIES

Although the trend for pregnancy jeans may have started with *thirtysomething*, it was difficult for women to be heavily pregnant and stylish in the 1980s since specialized maternity wear tended to be based on the tent. A lot of pregnancy fashion featured smocks or big shirts worn

*Left:* Actor Nastassja Kinski goes against the all-black trend of the late 1980s and early 1990s by wearing a colorful maternity kaftan in 1993.

with stretch-waisted pants or, for the later stages, loose, ethnic kaftans. Few women could afford to buy a wardrobe of maternity garments that would only be worn for nine months. Since it was hard to find anything stylish or flattering at a reasonable price in maternity stores, many women did not bother or just splurged on one or two pieces for a special occasion such as a wedding or an evening party.

However, as the 1990s progressed and more pregnant women continued to go out to work until they were close to term, there was a demand for more fashionable styles based on everyday, non-pregnant shapes (at least until the last two months, when disguise was no longer an option). The trend in maternity clothing during this period was increasingly to dress as usual for as long as possible. The idea of the yummy mommy, a woman whose interest in fashion was undimmed by the presence of children in her life, began to take shape. Soon, any garment was deemed acceptable for a pregnant woman as long as it didn't have a tight waist. Initially simple linen shifts and wrap-front jersey dresses were worn in place of strictly tailored skirts or pantsuits for work because dresses were much more flattering to the expanding figure than separates. Later on in the 1990s, however, pregnant women were seen sporting stretchy, close-fitting spandex tops that celebrated their growing bump.

In some ways, evening dress was an easier option for pregnant women since it was always possible to find sweeping dresses that had been designed for summer cruise wear. Flowing 1970s styles were rediscovered for formal occasions. Leisure wear was possibly the easiest option of all, thanks to stretch fabrics. Tracksuits and T-shirts could simply be purchased a size or two larger or just worn till they would stretch no more. In the 1980s, swimwear included one-piece costumes with a stretchy front panel, but by the end of the 1990s, braver mothers-to-be could be seen sporting bikinis.

## THE FAME GAME

During the 1980s and 1990s, the continuing success of celebrity and human-interest magazines such as *People* and *Hello!* fed the public a seemingly never-ending diet of interviews and color photographs. Some celebrities chose to announce news of important occasions in their lives, such as marriages and pregnancies, in these magazines. As the 1990s progressed, the Internet began to invade the territory previously dominated by celebrity magazines. By simply typing a few words into an

## THE CURSE OF CELEBRITY

" America churns out celebrities—real and pseudo—like high-fructose corn syrup, whether in the form of hot new 'It' actresses, reality TV rookie celebs, rich nobodies with image consultants, or scandalous girl-next-doors on YouTube. "

Erika Eichelberger, *New York Inquirer*, December 1, 2006

Internet search engine, a member of the public could quickly find out intimate details of a famous person's life. Meanwhile, the huge popularity of reality TV shows meant that ordinary people, with apparently little talent, could scale the dizzy heights of stardom. And the never-ending cycle of celebrity culture meant that the media, which had created the obsession and profited from it, were obliged to keep stoking it with more news and images.

## GLITZ, BLING, AND THE RED CARPET

The awards ceremony is one aspect of celebrity culture that has been around for many years. Movie and television awards ceremonies have long been influential showcases of fashion, with even the grandest of designers competing to lend their latest and most glamorous creations to adorn movie stars. A fashion house can gain thousands of dollars' worth of free publicity if it can convince stars such as Julia Roberts or Nicole Kidman to wear an evening dress from its collection to the Oscars ceremony. Even in 1990, a single full-page color advertisement in *Vogue* cost more than $20,000. It therefore makes perfect business sense for a designer to have his or her dress on the ultimate catwalk in Hollywood, in a show that is viewed by millions of people worldwide.

For the movie stars involved, an awards ceremony is the perfect excuse for dressing up in a big way, with the right dress definitely giving careers a boost. In 1994, at the London premier of the movie *Four Weddings and a Funeral*, British actor Elizabeth Hurley wore a striking, figure-hugging black dress by Gianni Versace. The eye-catching feature of this dress was that it was open down the sides and held together across the gaps with large gold safety pins. Hurley appeared on the red carpet alongside the movie's leading man, Hugh Grant, and the assembled press pack went wild. Her photograph

*Above:* Designers compete ferociously to get stars such as Nicole Kidman to wear their creations to the Oscars ceremony.

## MAKE IT—A SLASHED GOWN

Buy a simple sheath dress and some oversized safety pins or lengths of chain. Have a friend cut slashes into the dress while you're wearing it, exposing as much of your body as you dare. Choose to have a plunging back and front *or* a rising hemline— both at once tends to look tacky. Fasten where necessary with the pins or chains firmly stitched in place. Underwear should be minimal, perhaps a thong or G-string, and bare legs or hold-up stockings.

*Above*: In 1994, unknown actor Elizabeth Hurley made the front page when she arrived at a film premier wearing a revealing Versace gown.

appeared on every front page for weeks, and her personal career as a celebrity took off overnight. In contrast to this display of female extravagance, most male movie stars wear very conventional evening dress, even if it is an Armani suit, loaned to them under the same terms.

## MARRIAGE IN THE SPOTLIGHT

In 1981, the wedding of the Prince of Wales to Lady Diana Spencer started a trend for the minutely detailed chronicling and copying of such "fairy-tale" unions. For this royal wedding, the dress code was as formal

*Left:* The dress in the movie *Muriel's Wedding* (1994) had a sleeker outline than its 1980s equivalent, with a long bodice, narrow sleeves, and minimal jewelry.

and traditional as it was possible to be. Lady Diana's outfit was designed by Elizabeth and David Emanuel, and it was the ultimate little girl's dream dress, with huge puffed sleeves and a frilly neckline. The gown was made of silk taffeta, decorated with lace; it was hand-embroidered with 10,000 pearls and had a 25-ft (7.6-m) train. The bridesmaids wore miniature versions of the bride's dress, and the page boys wore frilled shirts and cream pants. This wedding set the bar for the next decade. Despite the fact that the dress looked like a meringue, it remained a hugely popular style. As the decade went on, sleeves of wedding dresses became narrower although they still kept a 1980s puffed shoulder. A longer bodice, fitted to the hips, became more typical.

## TRADITION

When a couple married in church, they tended to conform to the customs of the church, so covered shoulders and a veil were more usual during the 1980s and early 1990s. However, during the 1990s the popularity of the formal civil wedding ceremony freed up the dress code. By the end of the

1990s, many bridal gowns were based on a boned, strapless corset-like bodice with a long, billowing skirt, with a wreath of flowers or a jeweled coronet replacing the long veil.

## THE SPICE GIRLS

Formed in 1994, the girl band known as the Spice Girls epitomized the rocketing to fame of a group of unknown artists. The group's life span ran parallel to the course of celebrity culture throughout the 1990s (the Spice Girls finally disbanded in 2000). Hugely popular, their first release, "Spice," became the best-selling album ever by a female group, but critics suggested that marketing and merchandising, rather than talent, were at the heart of the band's success. The term "girl power," which was used to describe the band's apparent solidarity as "women warriors," was taken up as a mantra by millions of young girls, who also copied the Spice Girls' style of dress. The ultimate Spice Girls item of clothing was the Union Jack figure-hugging shift dress worn by Geri Halliwell, but other items

*Below:* The Spice Girls mixed old-fashioned show business glamour with edgier elements, such as brightly colored hairpieces, tattoos, and a feisty attitude.

included velvet shorts, glittery knee-length boots, catsuits, and platform shoes. The emphasis was on female strength, but this was usually presented in a conventionally sexy way.

In June 1997, the group began filming their movie debut, *Spiceworld: The Movie*, with director Bob Spiers. The style and content of the movie was intended to be in the same vein as the Beatles' films of the 1960s, such as *A Hard Day's Night*. It featured a range of stars, including Roger Moore, Hugh Laurie, Elton John, Jennifer Saunders, Richard E. Grant, Elvis Costello, and Meat Loaf. The movie was a minor hit at the box office but was not as popular with critics. It was nominated for seven awards at the 1999 Golden Raspberry Awards and "won" the award for Worst Actress.

## FRIENDS

In the 1990s, the cult of celebrity and its impact on the world of fashion hit new heights. The TV show *Friends*, which premiered in 1994, revolved around a group of six friends living together in Manhattan. Jennifer Aniston, who played the character of fashion enthusiast Rachel Green, became a fashion icon herself with a succession of slinky dresses, flirty miniskirts, and close-fitting sweaters. The bouncy, square, layered hairstyle worn by Aniston in the first season of the series was slavishly copied by many women in the 1990s and became so well known that it was referred to simply as "the Rachel."

*Below: Friends* in fashion—Jennifer Aniston (center) wears "the Rachel" haircut.

*Right:* Sarah Jessica Parker as Carrie in *Sex and the City*, complete with designer purse and signature corsage.

**COSTUMES AS CHARACTER**

"The clothes are like another character in the show. They help make it real."

Cynthia Nixon, who plays Miranda in the TV show *Sex and the City*, in an interview with *People* magazine

## SEX AND THE CITY

Fashion has never been so important in a TV show as it was in *Sex and the City*, a tale of four working women in search of romance and fulfilment in late 1990s Manhattan. Each character was defined by her clothes—from confident Samantha, in her startling red, skintight dresses and hoop earrings, to the bohemian Carrie, who mixed expensive designer shoes with thrift shop items to achieve a funky, original look—and women around the world mimicked their style.

Actor Sarah Jessica Parker, who played Carrie, was renowned for her sense of style and she hired costume designer Patricia Field, who scoured the international collections, couture shops, and thrift stores for inspiration. For each show, the wardrobe designers produced more than fifty outfits. Carrie's look demonstrated how mixing and matching could be used to great effect—by jumbling up colors, prints, accessories, and designer heels with a chain store dress or a pair of old jeans. Although Carrie was often costumed in glamorous Givenchy couture gowns and designer dresses from Dolce & Gabbana and Chanel, her character was given more "depth" by supplementing this look with thrift store finds, including floral sundresses and vibrant printed skirts. Carrie and her friends were also famous for their taste in expensive designer detailing, including sky-high stiletto sandals, mules, and pumps by Jimmy Choo or Manolo Blahnik, worn either with bare legs or with super-sheer pantyhose, and accompanied by designer purses and flower pins. Carrie's trademark accessories—from her glitzy gold "Carrie" chains to the ladylike corsages adorning her prim prom dresses—became must-haves for a generation of women.

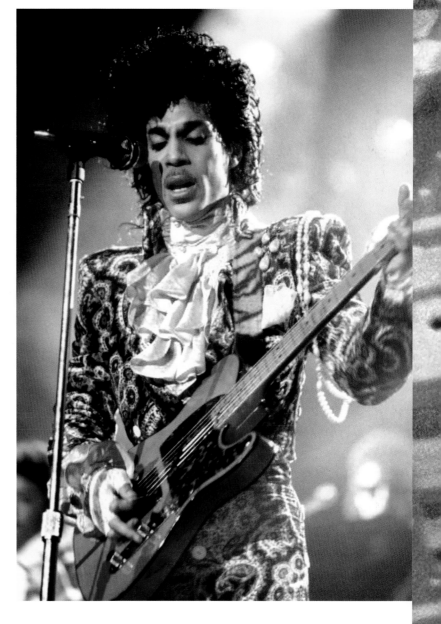

*Below:* Prince in full-on regal attire, combining luxurious brocade, satin, ruffles, and pearls.

## MEN GO ROYAL

The 1980s saw the rise to fame of Minneapolis-born rock performer Prince, whose music brought together a wide range of periods and styles, including rhythm and blues, soul, funk, jazz, and hip-hop. Like his music, Prince's stage costumes drew on a wide range of sources and his concerts were celebrated not just for his remarkable musicianship but for his habit of dressing in outrageous finery. In his 1984 movie, *Purple Rain*, for example, he wore clothes that were reminiscent of a hero from an eighteenth-century romantic novel: a ruffled, high-collared shirt and a purple trench coat with a deep back vent. He also favored asymmetrical ornamentation, such as diagonally buttoned flies on pants and chain mail detailing on the shoulder of a jacket. Like the New Romantics before him, Prince wore high heels and used makeup to project an ambiguous attitude toward conventional ideas of masculinity and femininity. The Prince look is an expensive one to attempt and necessitates a determined trawl of thrift stores until you find the brightest, shiniest, most sumptuous and highly decorated separates you can lay your hands on.

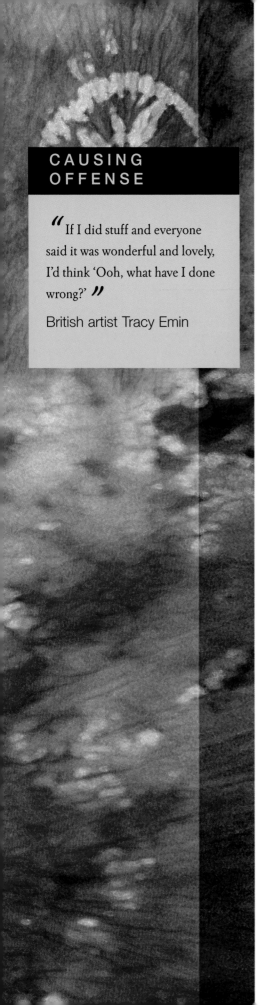

# CHAPTER 8

# Counterculture

## CAUSING OFFENSE

" If I did stuff and everyone said it was wonderful and lovely, I'd think 'Ooh, what have I done wrong?' "

British artist Tracy Emin

*Above:* The term *counterculture* describes any group with values different from those of mainstream society, including body-piercing enthusiasts.

## SHOCK TACTICS

By the 1990s, teens and young adults were faced with a dilemma: in a society where in clothing terms "anything goes," how do you make what you wear a statement of rebellion? As with so much else, music and art showed the way. Modern artists rejected the qualities that previous generations of artists had held in high regard. Conventionally "beautiful" works of art became objects of derision and abuse—to the confusion and distress of those not at the cutting edge. In the UK, a group of young British artists (YBAs) used shock tactics and disposable materials—with works featuring pickled sharks and soiled, unmade beds—and gained a huge amount of media coverage in the process.

This impulse to offend also expressed itself in fashion, where dressing to shock had always been a sure way to get a rise from parents and anyone in authority. The 1990s saw an explosion in multiple body piercings, tattoos, and extreme hair—either shaved or arranged in towering, increasingly matted dreadlocks. Metal rings poked through eyebrows, navels, noses, and even tongues and ranged like buttons down breastbones—pain, it seemed, was no deterrent. Completely shaved hair on women—once the ultimate badge of shame—was another fashion shock tactic. Torn jeans and ripped undershirts completed the look.

## GRUNGE

In 1993, a photo session for *Vogue* magazine featured a skinny teenage model from Croydon, England. These pictures of the young Kate Moss caused a sensation. For a start, there was no attempt to make her look glamorous in any normal sense of the word. She was photographed in her underwear in an ordinary apartment, with apparently natural lighting. She looked unhealthy and underweight, as if hung over from some excesses of the night before.

If there had been any doubts that each decade produces fashions to counter those of the previous decade, then the 1990s swept them away. There could not have been a starker contrast to the tanned, powerful Californian models of the 1980s than that of the "superwaif." The new style was known as "grunge." With its roots in Seattle, grunge was primarily a music genre that took its inspiration from hard-core punk, heavy metal, and indie rock. Like punk, grunge lyrics were concerned with social alienation and injustice, but unlike punk, they were angst-ridden rather than angry. They reflected a culture in which young

*Right:* Kate Moss and Johnny Depp, managing to look grungy yet stylish in 1995.

people felt trapped and depressed about the future. Grunge costume consisted of thrift store items, outdoor-type clothing (particularly flannel shirts), and a generally unkempt appearance.

Capitalizing on the new trend, the fashion industry marketed "grunge fashion" to consumers, charging premium prices for items such as knit ski hats. Critics accused advertisers of co-opting elements of grunge and turning it into a fad. Unlike the supermodels of the 1980s, Kate Moss wasn't defined entirely by the couture clothes she wore on the catwalk but instead quickly became a personality or celebrity in her own right, with her own style. Her "look" was often related to and reflected by her boyfriend of the moment, in the early days actor Johnny Depp and later

*Right:* Seattle band Alice in Chains wearing the jeans, T-shirts, and big sunglasses beloved of grunge.

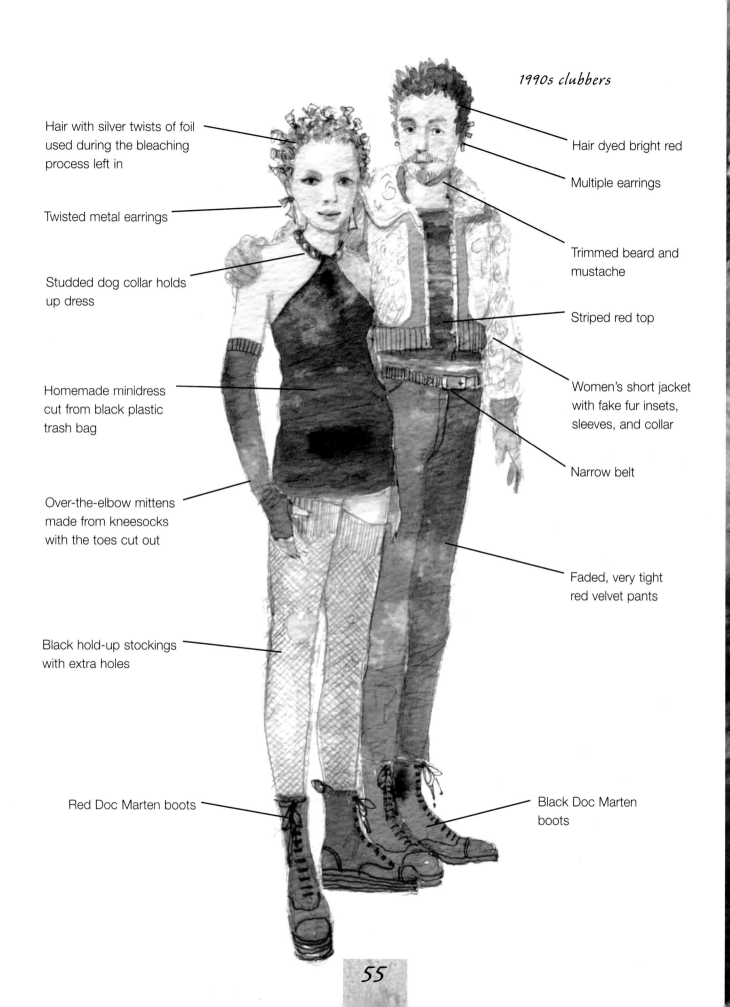

Hair with silver twists of foil used during the bleaching process left in

Twisted metal earrings

Studded dog collar holds up dress

Homemade minidress cut from black plastic trash bag

Over-the-elbow mittens made from kneesocks with the toes cut out

Black hold-up stockings with extra holes

Red Doc Marten boots

Hair dyed bright red

Multiple earrings

Trimmed beard and mustache

Striped red top

Women's short jacket with fake fur insets, sleeves, and collar

Narrow belt

Faded, very tight red velvet pants

Black Doc Marten boots

55

singer-songwriter Pete Doherty. Moss's lifestyle, which included the use of alcohol, cocaine, and cigarettes as well as arrests for drug possession and stays in the more exclusive rehab establishments, also served to underline the notion that it was no longer "cool" to be "sweet."

### GEEK CHIC

The year 1996 brought "geek chic." With some embarrassment, a *Vogue* editorial of the time stated that purple Crimplene slacks, shirts in shower-curtain-printed nylon, plaid A-line miniskirts, flat shoes, and plastic lunch boxes as purses constituted fashionable urban wear for the style-conscious young. These clothes were intentionally ironic, or "off." The idea was that, as with grunge fashion, it was un-cool to look too attractive or stylish. Unfortunately for the purveyors of such deliberate nerdiness, people outside the fashion world loop tended to think that this look was just plain unattractive, and it failed to enter the mainstream culture.

*Above:* Tall and awkward but with an eye for fashion, Jarvis Cocker of the British band Pulp perfected the geek chic look.

### COUNTERCULTURAL STIRRINGS

Fashion trends at the end of the 1990s were an assortment of many things—there was no single, defining shape. In an attempt to impose a single 1990s style on an increasingly fragmented fashion world, this confused situation was described in fashion magazines as "the Supermarket of Style" or even "the Gathering of the Tribes."

One consistent influence on fashion throughout the 1980s and 1990s was the rapidly growing culture of the music festival. The first large outdoor music festival was probably Woodstock in the United States in "the Summer of Love" of 1967, but the movement really took off in the early 1980s with the establishment of Glastonbury in the UK, now one of the biggest music festivals in the world. By the end of the 1990s, many other festivals had sprung into being. At these events, music was still an important feature, but the driving force behind them was people's need to express, and experience, an alternative lifestyle. Many people were appalled by what they saw as the consumerist, celebrity-obsessed capitalist society of the latter part of the twentieth century. They were also increasingly aware of the damage humans were doing to the environment and angry and disillusioned with the ability or will of politicians to make a difference.

Music festivals brought together many "single-issue" activists, including those in the green movement, eco-warriors, New Age travelers, and practitioners of all kinds of alternative therapies. Previously, these groups had been dismissed as the lunatic fringe, but with growing fears about global warming and the world energy crisis, many people began to think that maybe it wasn't so crazy after all to put the planet first and have a good time while you were at it.

*Left:* Boiler suits, florals, and hiking boots at Woodstock in 1994.

## HIP THREADS

Web sites offering festival clothes for sale often advertise garments made to green, ethical standards. They include knitwear, such as sweaters, jackets, ponchos, shawls, hats, scarves, gloves, and mittens; hand-dyed and appliquéd T-shirts and skirts; handmade hemp jewelry; yoga wear, kids' clothes—anything, in fact, that the modern hippie could want or need. The irony of the use of aggressive merchandising techniques by many of the sites won't escape the more earnest and ethically aware members of the festival-going set!

## FESTIVAL CHIC

Not surprisingly, the dress code for festival goers owed much to the hippie era of the 1960s, only the newer participant was more suntanned and had bigger boots (often tall rubber boots or the military-style Doc Martens). Most festival goers wore a colorful mixture of garments gleaned from thrift shops and eco-stores, together with ethnic bits and pieces, either Indian or South American in origin. Women wore long skirts made from old saris with tight, tie-dyed tops and multiple necklaces of glass or wood beads. The men wore patched and faded jeans and either T-shirts and vests or bright collarless shirts from India or Guatemala. Men's jewelry included a range of wood and shell necklaces. Children were always present at festivals, especially at the less music-based venues such as the Burning Man Festival in Nevada. A special festival fashion particularly popular with little girls consisted of fairy dresses with sparkly ballet skirts and wings. "Festival chic" became a new style, with fashion leaders such as Kate Moss arriving at Glastonbury in a short summery dress or cutoff shorts, worn with a tight leather jacket and rubber boots.

*Below:* The pick 'n' mix culture of the 1990s meant that, by this point, almost any combination of dress styles was acceptable.

58

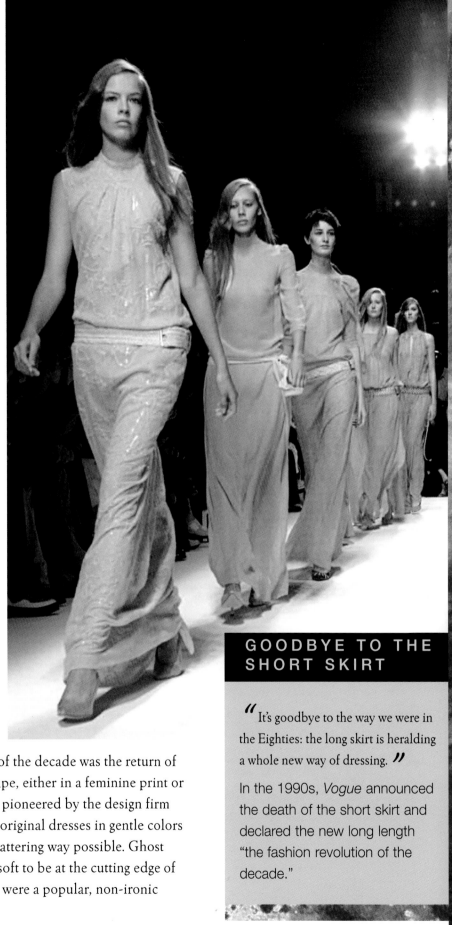

*Right:* In 1999, design company Ghost breaks away from fashion's obsession with black with a collection in subtle pastel shades.

## TOWARD THE MILLENNIUM

As the 1990s drew to a close, the outline of women's wear became far softer: shoulder pads shrank in size, then disappeared entirely and little cardigans and bias-cut garments replaced oversized jackets and straight skirts. Fashion became more fluid, and hemlines rose and fell indecisively year after year.

After the long, dark years of the late 1980s, when black dominated the fashion scene, color returned in a big way during the 1990s with dazzling acid-drop hues as bright as chemical dyes could make them. However, although bright block colors and retro prints were wildly fashionable, many women couldn't give up their preference for black. Perversely, members of the fashion world wore more black than anyone at this time, as did costume people in film and theater. And the "little black dress," or "LBD," so beloved by stylish women for cocktail parties, remained very popular.

The other trend during the last years of the decade was the return of the day dress, often in a simple wrap shape, either in a feminine print or in the figure-hugging, honeycomb rayon pioneered by the design firm Ghost. These were beautiful and highly original dresses in gentle colors that accentuated the figure in the most flattering way possible. Ghost dresses were possibly too feminine and soft to be at the cutting edge of late-twentieth-century fashion, but they were a popular, non-ironic alternative to grunge and geek.

## GOODBYE TO THE SHORT SKIRT

*" It's goodbye to the way we were in the Eighties: the long skirt is heralding a whole new way of dressing. "*

In the 1990s, *Vogue* announced the death of the short skirt and declared the new long length "the fashion revolution of the decade."

# Glossary

**acetate** Short for acetate rayon, a synthetic fiber.

**androgyny** A state of having both male and female characteristics.

**atelier** A French word meaning "studio" or "workshop"; a designer's workroom where designs are created and made up.

**bandanna** A large patterned handkerchief worn round the head or neck.

**Barbour jacket** An English country weather coat made from waterproof waxed cotton.

**basque** (1) A short flared piece of fabric attached to the bodice at the waist. (2) A fitted hip piece on women's pants.

**bat-wing sleeve** A long sleeve with an armhole cut to the waist and narrow at the wrist.

**bodice** The part of a dress from the shoulder to the waist.

**bohemian chic** An unconventional, thrift store arty style of dress, popular in the 1990s.

**bouclé** A looped yarn or fabric, giving a thick knobbly effect.

**brocade** A rich, stiff silk fabric with a pattern woven into it.

**bustier** A close-fitting, strapless, sleeveless top.

**camisole** A light under-bodice with a straight-cut top on narrow shoulder straps.

**capitalist** Describes an economic system based on private ownership of business and trade.

**chambray** A light cotton fabric with a white weft and a colored warp.

**chiffon** Transparent floaty fabric woven from silk, rayon, or polyester.

**classic** Clothing that remains stylish because of its essential simplicity; not dependent on passing trends.

**corsage** A bouquet of real or artificial flowers worn as decoration at the shoulder, breast, or waist.

**corset** A figure-molding, supportive undergarment, stiffened with plastic strips.

**cotton lawn** A fine cotton fabric, probably named for Laon, a town in France where linen was made.

**couture** French for "dressmaking"; used to mean the top or made-to-measure end of the fashion spectrum.

**couturier** A top international fashion designer.

**crepe de chine** A very light silk or cotton fabric with a wrinkled surface.

**epaulettes** Ornamental shoulder pieces.

**espadrille** A rope-soled shoe with a canvas upper, for casual summer wear.

**haute couture** High fashion, always made to measure.

**jersey** A cotton or cotton-blend knitted fabric.

**Liberty print** A collection of fabrics, often floral in design, named for the Liberty store in London, UK.

**loafer** A casual slip-on shoe with a low heel, based on the moccasin.

**materialism** An excessive interest in making money or accumulating possessions.

**minimalist** Being or providing a bare minimum of what is necessary.

**preppy** A style of neat, understated, and often expensive clothes.

**serge** A twill fabric, usually of wool or worsted, with a diagonal ribbed texture.

**taffeta** A thin, crisp fabric of silk or rayon.

**tweed** A closely woven, unfinished wool fabric with a rough texture, originating in Scotland.

## BOOKS

Clancy, Deirdre. *Costume Since 1945: Couture, Street Style and Anti-Fashion.* Drama Publishers, 1996.

Harrison, Martin. *Parkinson's Photographs, 1935 to 1990.* Conran Octopus, 1994.

Howell, Georgina. *In Vogue: Seventy-five Years of Style.* Conde Nast/Century, 1991.

McDowell, Colin. *McDowell's Directory of 20th-Century Fashion.* Muller, 1994.

Polhemus, Ted. *Street Style.* Thames & Hudson, 1994.

Poli, Doretta Davanzo. *Maternity Fashion.* Zanfi Editori, 1988.

Wenborn, Neil. *Hamlyn Pictorial History of the 20th Century.* Bounty Books, 1999.

## WEB SITES

www.fashionera.com/1980s_lifestyle_and_fashion.htm
Web site with 710 illustrated pages about women's fashion, costume, and social history. Special features on New Romantics, power dressing, haute couture, and body adornment,

www.fashion-era.com/the_1990s.htm
Similar to the preceding web site, with features on minimalist fashion, Donna Karan, pashminas, and dressing down.

http://fashion.about.com/cs/celebtrendsetters/a/sexandcitystyle.htm
Advice on how to go about getting that *SATC* style.

http://eightiesclub.tripod.com/an_encyclopedia_of_the_1980_s.htm
An online encyclopedia about the 1980s with information about the Brat Pack, yuppie culture, and Madonna.

www.experiencefestival.com/1990s_fashion_-_grunge_amp_retro-hippie
An archive on 1990s fashion, with articles on grunge and retro hippie styles.

www.liketotally80s.com/80s-fashion.html
Youth fashion site with ideas for retro dressing, including hairstyles and accessories.

## AMERICAN FESTIVALS

**Bean Blossom**
www.beanblossom.com/
Bean Blossom, Brown County, Indiana
A bluegrass, gospel, and blues festivals held throughout summer and fall.

**Bonnaroo Music and Arts Festival**
www.bonnaroo.com/
Manchester, Tennessee
A four-day multi-stage camping festival.

**Bumbershoot**
www.bumbershoot.org/
Seattle Center, Seattle, Washington
A music and arts festival.

**The Burning Man Festival**
www.burningman.com/
Black Rock Desert, Nevada
A spontaneous community, art installation, and theme camp.

**Newport Folk Festival**
www.festivalnetwork.com/
Newport, Rhode Island
A folk, country, and blues festival.

**San Francisco LoveFest**
www.sflovefest.org/
Newport, Rhode Island
The largest single-day electronic dance music event in America.

# Source List

A selection of movies and TV series with 1980s and 1990s themes.

## THE EIGHTIES

### MOVIES

*Baby Boom* (1987), dir. Charles Shyer, with Diane Keaton, Harold Ramis

*Big* (1988), dir. Penny Marshall, with Tom Hanks, Elizabeth Perkins

*The Big Chill* (1983), dir. Lawrence Kasdan, with Tom Berenger, Glenn Close

*The Breakfast Club* (1985), dir. John Hughes, with Emilio Estevez, Judd Nelson

*A Chorus Line* (1985), dir. Richard Attenborough, with Michael Douglas, Terrence Mann

*Desperately Seeking Susan* (1985), dir. Susan Seidelman, with Rosanna Arquette, Madonna

*Fame* (1980), dir. Alan Parker, with Irene Cara, Lee Curreri

*Fatal Attraction* (1987), dir. Adrian Lyne, with Michael Douglas, Glenn Close

*Ferris Bueller's Day Off* (1986), dir. John Hughes, with Mathew Broderick, Alan Ruck

*Flashdance* (1983), dir. Adrian Lyne, with Jennifer Beals, Michael Nouri

*Footloose* (1984), dir. Herbert Ross, with Kevin Bacon, Lori Singer

*Heathers* (1988), dir. Michael Lehmann, with Winona Ryder, Christian Slater

*The Karate Kid* (1984), dir. John G. Avildsen, with Ralph Macchio, Noriyuki "Pat" Morita

*Less Than Zero* (1987), dir. Marek Kanievska, with Andrew McCarthy, Jami Gertz

*Nine to Five* (1980), dir. Colin Higgins, with Jane Fonda, Dolly Parton

*An Officer and a Gentleman* (1982), dir. Taylor Hackford, with Richard Gere, Debra Winger

*Pretty in Pink* (1986), dir. John Hughes, with Molly Ringwald, Harry Dean Stanton

*The Princess Bride* (1987), dir. Rob Reiner, with Cary Elwes, Mandy Patinkin

*Purple Rain* (1984), dir. Albert Magnoli, with Prince, Apollonia Kotero

*Risky Business* (1983), dir. Paul Brickman, with Tom Cruise, Rebecca de Mornay

*Stand by Me* (1986), dir. Rob Reiner, with Wil Wheaton, River Phoenix

*Steel Magnolias* (1989), dir. Herbert Ross, with Sally Field, Dolly Parton

*St. Elmo's Fire* (1985), dir. Joel Schumacher, with Rob Lowe, Demi Moore

*Subway* (1985), dir. Luc Besson, with Christophe Lambert, Isabelle Adjani

*Three Men and a Baby* (1987), dir. Leonard Nimoy, with Ted Danson, Tom Selleck

*Top Gun* (1986), dir. Tony Scott, with Tom Cruise, Kelly McGillis

*Wall Street* (1987), dir. Oliver Stone, with Michael Douglas, Charlie Sheen

*Weird Science* (1985), dir. John Hughes, with Anthony Michael Hall, Kelly Le Brock

*Working Girl* (1988), dir. Mike Nichols, with Harrison Ford, Melanie Griffith

### TV

*Cheers* (1982–93), with Ted Danson, Rhea Perlman

*The Cosby Show* (1984–92), with Bill Cosby, Phylicia Rashad

*Dallas* (1978–91), with Larry Hagman, Patrick Duffy

*Dynasty* (1981–9), with John Forsythe, Joan Collins

*Growing Pains* (1985–92), with Alan Thicke, Joanna Kerns

*Hill Street Blues* (1981–7), with Daniel J. Travanti, Bruce Weitz

*Miami Vice* (1984–9), with Don Johnson, Philip Michael Thomas

*thirtysomething* (1987–91), with Ken Olin, Mel Harris

*21 Jump Street* (1987–91), with Steven Williams, Johnny Depp

## THE NINETIES

### MOVIES

*Boys on the Side* (1995), dir. Herbert Ross, with Whoopi Goldberg, Mary-Louise Parker

*Clueless* (1995), dir. Amy Heckerling, with Alicia Silverstone, Stacey Dash

*Four Weddings and a Funeral* (1994), dir. Mike Newell, with Hugh Grant, Andie MacDowell

*Ghost* (1990), dir. Jerry Zucker, with Patrick Swayze, Demi Moore

*Muriel's Wedding* (1994), dir. P. J. Hogan, with Toni Collette, Rachel Griffiths

*My Best Friend's Wedding* (1997), dir. P. J. Hogan, with Julia Roberts, Dermot Mulroney

*Pulp Fiction* (1994), dir. Quentin Tarantino, with John Travolta, Samuel L. Jackson

*Pretty Woman* (1990), dir. Garry Marshall, with Richard Gere, Julia Roberts

*Romy and Michele's High School Reunion* (1997), dir. David Mirkin, with Mira Sorvino, Lisa Kudrow

*Sleepless in Seattle* (1993), dir. Nora Ephron, with Tom Hanks, Meg Ryan

*Spice World: The Movie* (1997), dir. Bob Spiers, with Geri Halliwell, Victoria Beckham

*Strictly Ballroom* (1992), dir. Baz Luhrmann, with Paul Mercurio, Tara Morice

*10 Things I Hate About You (*1999), dir. Gil Junger, with Heath Ledger, Julia Stiles

*Thelma and Louise* (1991), dir. Ridley Scott, with Susan Sarandon, Geena Davis

*The Truth About Cats and Dogs* (1996), dir. Michael Lehmann, with Uma Thurman, Janeane Garofalo

*Walking and Talking* (1996), dir. Nicole Holofcener, with Catherine Keener, Anne Heche

*Wayne's World* (1992), dir. Penelope Spheeris, with Mike Myers, Dana Carvey

*You've Got Mail* (1998), dir. Nora Ephron, with Tom Hanks, Meg Ryan

### TV

*Frasier* (1993–2004), with Kelsey Grammer, David Hyde Pierce

*The Fresh Prince of Bel-Air* (1990–96), with Will Smith, Alfonso Ribeiro

*Friends* (1994–2004), with Jennifer Aniston, David Schwimmer

*Roseanne* (1989–97), with Roseanne Barr, John Goodman

*Seinfeld* (1989–1998), with Jerry Seinfeld, Michael Richards

*Sex and the City* (1998–2004), with Sarah Jessica Parker, Kim Cattrall

Numbers in **bold** refer to illustrations.

accessories **11**, **13**, 14, 25, 40, 50, **50**, 51
advertising 20, 21, 24, 40, 43, 45

beading 10, **11**, 13, 17, 22
bikers 38, **38-9**, 40
body piercing 52, **52**, 53

catalogs 5, 29, 30
celebrities 44-5, **45**, 46, **46**, 48-9, **48-9**, **53**, 54
cell phones 7, 24, 25
coats 9, 13, **13**, 21, 27, 40, 43, 51
colors 9, 14, **14**, 18, **18**, 22, 25, 34, 37, 38, 50, 59
corsets 36, 38, 41, **41**
couture 5, 7, **7**, 8, **9**, 13, **13**, 20-23, **20-23**, 29, 41, 50, 54
couturiers 5, **7**, 8, **9**, 13, **13**, 16, 18, 20-23, **20-23**, 36, 45, 50

Diana, Princess 14, **15**, 16, **16**, 46-7
dresses 10, 13, **13**, 14, **14**, 16, 17, **40**, 41, 44, 45, 46, 47, **47**, 48, 49, 50, 51, **55**, 58, 59, **59**

evening wear 10, **10-11**, 13, 14, 16, **16**, 20, 22, 41, 44, 45, **45**, 46, **46**

fashion
  designers *see* couturiers
  models **7**, **9**, 18-19, **19**, **20**, **21**, 38, 40, **40**, 53, **53**, 54
  1980s 7, **7**, 8, **8**, 9, **9**, 10, **10-19**, 12-14, 16-18, 20-23, **20-23**, **24-5**, 25, 26-7, **26-7**, 28-9, **28**, 30, 32-4, **32**, **34**, 35, 36-7, **36-7**, **42-3**
  1990s 7, 8, 26, 28, 29, **29**, 30, **30**, **31**, 33, **33**, 34, 35, 44-5, **44-5**, 48-51, **48-51**, 52-9, **52-9**
festivals 56-8, **57**
footwear **11**, 14, **15**, 18, 21, 25, 26, 27, 29, **29**, 30, **31**, 33, 37, 38, **39**, 40, 49, 50, 51, 53, **55**, 56, **57**, 58
*Friends* 38, 49, **49**

geek chic 56, **56**
gloves 17, 40, 58
goths 38
grunge 8, 53-4, **54**, 56

hairstyles 9, 10, **10**, **11**, 14, **15**, 18, 22, 27, **27**, **31**, **36**, 37, 38, **39**, 40, **48**, 49, **49**, 53, **55**
hats 13, **13**, 16, 26, **39**, 40, 54, 58
high fashion *see* couture

jackets 8, 9, **9**, 14, **14**, 18, 26, 27, **27**, 28, **31**, 34, 38, **39**, 40, 41, 50, 51, **55**, 58, 59
jeans 9, 21, 26, 27, **27**, 28, **28**, 29, 30, **39**, 40, 43, 50, 51, 53, **54**
jewelry 10, **10**, **11**, 14, 16, 17, **17**, 22, **31**, 38, 40, 50, 53, **55**, 58

lace 38, 47
leather 38, 40, 41, 53, 58
leggings 33, 53
leg warmers **32**, 33
Lycra 21, 32, 33, 34

Madonna 16-18, **17**, 41, **41**
makeup **11**, 17, **31**, 37, **37**, 38, 40, 51, 53
maternity wear 43, 44, **44**
men's wear 18, **18**, 21, 22, 24, 25-7, **24-7**, 28, **28**, **30**, **31**
*Miami Vice* 18, **18**, 26
Moss, Kate 20, 53, **53**, 54, 56, 58
movies 5, 17, **24-5**, 33, 35, 42, **42**, 45, **45**, 46, **46**, **47**, 49

New Romantics 37, **37**, 51
night wear 35, **35**
nylon 34, 56

pants 9, 18, **21**, 22, 26, 27, 28, **31**, 34, 37, 40, 44, 47, 51, 53, **55**
pantsuits 25, 44
pantyhose **11**, 16, 17, 25, **31**, 51
*People* 5, 44, 50
popular music **5**, 8, **27**, 38, 53, **54**, **56**
punks 22, **36**, 37, **38**, 53
purses 9, 14, 22, **50**, 51, 56

Reagan, Nancy 12, 13, **13**
rock chicks 38, **38**, 40

satin 10, 35, 41, **51**
*Sex and the City* 50-51, **50**
shell suits 33-4, **34**
shirts 9, 14, **15**, 21, 22, 25, 26, 27, 28, 37, 43, 51, **51**, 54, 56, 58
shorts 33, 49, 58
shoulder pads 7, 8, 9, **9**, 10, 13, 21, 26, 59
silk 10, 13, 14, **16**, 34, 35, 41, 47
skirts 9, **9**, 10, 14, **15**, 16, 17, 21, 27, 29, **31**, 40, 41, 44, 49, 50, 51, 53, 56, 58, 59
sleeves 10, **11**, 13, 16, 17, 47, **47**
spandex 21, 32, 33, 34, 44
Spice Girls 48-9, **48**
sportswear 29, 32-4, **32-4**
St. Laurent, Yves **7**, 22, **22**, 25, 41
street fashion 5, 22, 36-9, **36-9**, 41
suits 8, 9, **9**, 14, 16, **18**, 21, 22, 24, 25, 26, **26**, 27, **38**, 43, 46

taffeta 10, 14, **16**, 47
tattoos **39**, 53
television shows **6**, 12, **12**, 18, **18**, **28**, 30, **32**, 37, 38, 43, **43**, 45, **49**, 50, **50**
Thatcher, Margaret 5, 13-14, **14**
thrift stores 7, 8, 26, 30, 50, 51, 54,
T-shirts 9, 16, 17, 18, 23, 28, 35, 37, 38, **39**, 40, 44, **54**, 58
tweed 14, 21, 26, 41

underwear 20, 21, 32, 33, 34, 35, 41

Versace, Gianni 21, **21**, 45, 46
*Vogue* 5, 19, 45, 53, 56, 59

weddings 41, 46-8, **47**
Westwood, Vivienne 22-3, 36, 37, **40**, 41
women's wear **7**, 9, **9**, 10, 12-17, **10-17**, 20-23, **20-23**, 24-5, **24**, 27, **28**, **29**, 30, **30**, **31**, 59, **59**

yummy mommies 44
yuppies 24, 43, **43**